OVERCOMING

FEAR OF DEATH

OVERCOMING FEAR OF DEATH

by

Richard J. Gehman

OASIS INTERNATIONAL LIMITED

Satisfying Africa's Thirst for God's Word

Overcoming Fear of Death

ISBN 13: 978-1-59452-727-2
ISBN: 1-59452-727-X

Published by Oasis International Ltd, in partnership with Richard J. Gehman. Oasis International is a ministry devoted to fostering a robust and sustainable pan-African publishing industry. Oasis has exclusive rights to publish and sell this work throughout the world. For more information, go to oasisint.net.

CONTENTS

PREFACE

In 1999 Evangel Publishing House published my 350 page book, *Who are the Living Dead: A Theology of Death, Life after Death and the Living Dead*. It is still in print and explores in depth the topics detailed in the sub-title.

Overcoming Fear of Death is a sequel to the 1999 publication. It arises out of two felt needs which have been shared by numerous pastors.

During those years when the Theological Advisory Group (TAG) was functioning in Kenya within the Africa Inland Church (1985-2000), dozens of pastors and church leaders offered their advice, saying that a great need for the Christian Church in Africa was a comprehensive treatment of salvation presented for the African context. Few African Christians, they said, understood the rich, deep, biblical truths of salvation. TAG never did engage that topic and to my knowledge nothing of substance has been published for lay people on the topic of salvation according to the Scriptures in the African context.

On numerous other occasions pastors shared their belief that the reason why Christians often lapse back into African Traditional Religion during times of sickness and death is because they do not have a full grasp of their salvation. Not being secure in their relationship with Jesus Christ and not understanding the priceless privileges they have as a child of God – adopted by the God the Father into the family of God, saved by the Lord Jesus Christ who died for them, and indwelled by the Holy Spirit who guarantees their salvation – they panic and fear, whenever trouble arises, and lapse back into their old religious beliefs and practices.

Within African traditional culture sickness and death are not chance accidents. They happen because others, through jealousy or enmity, have used witchcraft or sorcery to strike at the wellbeing of their enemy. Or it may be that the ancestral spirits have been displeased with their neglect and disregard for ancestral traditions. To learn the exact nature of the problem, the traditional solution was to consult a specialist – a diviner – to determine the cause and solution.

In many African communities the fears of mystical powers run deep. Whatever problems arise – famine, accidents, sickness, infertility, miscarriage, or crop failure – attention is directed to malevolent persons, living or dead. Sorcery, witchcraft, witches, curses, evil eye, evil tongue, black magic or any other form of mystical powers are thought to be the cause. And this leads to heightened fear and horror.

That fear arises among unbelieving Africans should surprise no one. But when Christians find themselves deeply anxious and troubled over misfortunes that occur, and when they fear the malicious intent of persons, living or the living-dead, this should arouse great concern for the Christian Church.

The purpose of this book is to deal with both of these issues: (1) provide a comprehensive exposition of salvation in the African context, (2) in order to grow Christians into spiritual maturity so that they will be enabled by God through his Word to stand strong and brave in the face of the many troubles, sickness and death which are common to the human race.

The solution to the fear of death is found in the Scriptures. For this reason the book is filled with passages of Scripture that teach basic truths of salvation. The reader should not be primarily concerned with what the author says. The question is, "What does the Scripture teach?"

We have numerous Bible translations in English. Some are more literal, word for word, translations while others are paraphrases which convey the thoughts expressed in the original language in popular, contemporary English. Throughout the book these different translations are used in order to clarify and elucidate the biblical teaching in contemporary English.

For more than sixty years the author has been studying, teaching and preaching these truths, and yet the preparation for this book continues to prove deeply enriching and edifying. God has provided us with such a marvelous salvation in Jesus Christ which needs to be embraced with ever deepening faith and devotion.

You may be a lay person without Bible training. This book was written for you. Or you may have gone to Bible School or College and you think that you know all about salvation. The truth is, we never know all that there is to know. Furthermore, God needs to write these truths more deeply in our hearts. As we continue to meditate on God's Word, the Holy Spirit edifies us and builds us up in the faith. The life of every Christian will be greatly strengthened through a re-examination of what God teaches concerning our great salvation proffered by God.

The author would encourage the reader to take out his or her vernacular Bible and use it when studying through these biblical truths. Nothing speaks to the depths of one's soul like the mother tongue, so combine the study of this book in English with the study of the vernacular Bible.

Christians can stand strong and fearless in the face of sickness and death. This book seeks to help the reader know the biblical teaching that strengthens faith to overcome fear of sickness and death.

ACKNOWLEDGEMENT

A hearty thanks is extended to my many African friends and colleagues in ministry who have made this book possible. Without the many lessons learned from them, especially through my observation, this book would not have been possible.

Although my wife and I poured our lives into teaching, discipling, researching, writing and a host of other ministries while in Kenya for 36 years, I have concluded that my African brothers and sisters have taught me more than I ever taught them. One important lesson was a spirit of humility, recognizing our commonality in both our humanity and in our unity in Christ.

Human beings are more alike than different. Not only do we share the same blood, we are all made in the image of God and experience the same effects of sin. We all share common needs, fears, hopes and dreams. As brothers and sisters in Christ we grow together in mutual understanding and respect. We are bonded together in love. To each one who impacted my life and helped shape this book, a hearty thanks.

As mentioned in the Preface, this book would never have been written if it were not for the frequent recommendations from the Theological Advisory Group and pastors over the years. We trust this book will meet an urgent need.

After writing the first draft of this book, it was sent to several individuals to read and critique. Dr. Alfred Muli went beyond the call of duty in carefully scrutinizing the content and making recommendations, even suggesting that one chapter be rewritten. Through his advice significant improvements have hopefully been made.

Dr. Keith Ferdinando, Rev. Elias Ng'etich, and Dr. Paul Balisky poured over the script and made helpful corrections and suggestions. For this I am thankful.

My deepest gratitude is to our Father in Heaven who has shepherded me over my lifetime. The thoughts expressed in this book come from a heart that has been nourished for decades by the Word of God. It could not have been written in the 1960s when we first went to Kenya. We knew not the African context at all and we knew not the Scriptures to the extent that we understand them today, especially as it applies to the context of African faith.

May the Lord be pleased to bless this effort for the strengthening of the Christian faith in Africa!

ABBREVIATIONS

Abbreviations for the Books of the Bible

Genesis — Ge	Isaiah — Isa	Romans — Ro
Exodus — Ex	Jeremiah — Jer	1 Corinthians — 1 Co
Leviticus —Lev	Lamentations – La	2 Corinthians — 2 Co
Numbers — Nu	Ezekiel — Eze	Galatians — Gal
Deuteronomy — Dt	Daniel — Da	Ephesians — Eph
Joshua — Jos	Hosea —Hos	Philippians — Php
Judges — Jdg	Joel —Joel	Colossians —Col
Ruth — Ru	Amos —Am	1 Thessalonians 1 Th
1 Samuel — 1 Sa	Obadiah — Ob	2 Thessalonians 2 Th
2 Samuel — 2 Sa	Jonah — Jnh	1 Timothy — 1 Ti
1 Kings — 1 Ki	Micah — Mic	2 Timothy — 2 Ti
2 Kings — 2 Ki	Nahum —Na	Titus —Tit
1 Chronicles — 1 Ch	Habakkuk —Hab	Philemon — Phm
2 Chronicles — 2 Ch	Zephaniah — Zep	Hebrews — Heb
Ezra — Ezr	Haggai — Hag	James — Jas
Nehemiah — Ne	Zechariah — Zec	1 Peter — 1 Pe
Esther — Est	Malachi — Mal	2 Peter — 2 Pe
Job — Job	Matthew — Mt	1 John — 1 Jn
Psalms — Ps	Mark — Mk	2 John — 2 Jn
Proverbs — Pr	Luke — Lk	3 John — 3 Jn
Ecclesiastes — Ecc	John — Jn	Jude — Jude
Song of Solomon SS	Acts — Ac	Revelation — Rev

1

UNIVERSAL
FEAR OF DEATH

Death haunts the human race around the globe. Everyone faces inevitable death and in some measure everyone fears it. This self-evident reality needs no proof from scientific investigation. Both educated and illiterate among all races show this fear. It can be seen by what they say and do; or by what they don't say and do. Death is an extra-ordinarily sensitive topic that most people shun.

The author took a manuscript to a publisher in the 1990s. When the woman looked at the title, her whole body shuddered and shook as she exclaimed, "Too much death!" The title and the book cover said it all: *Who are the Living-Dead? A Theology of Death, Life after Death and the Living Dead*. The cover portrayed ghostly figures. They refused to publish it.

EVIDENCE OF UNIVERSAL FEAR

Anthropologist Ernest Becker argues that "the idea of death, the fear of it, haunts the human animal like nothing else; it is the mainspring of human activity – activity designed largely to avoid the fatality of death, to overcome it by denying in some way that it is the final destiny for man."[1]

Calvin Moore states that "Death, in all its complexity, finality, and absurdity, its challenge to existence, its ugliness, pain, and isolation, and its power to deprive, continues to hold sway over humankind."[2]

Evidence for death rites can be found in gravesites thousands of years ago. The cult of the dead can be traced to the beginning of the Old Stone Age when people buried flint knives, food and relics associated with special ceremonies for the dead. Death rites are universal and were performed in antiquity past, revealing the crisis that always accompanies the end of life. These rites not only enable people to express their grief in a culturally acceptable way, the rites serve as a means of restoring social balance among the living after someone is snatched from them. The meaning and

---

[1] Moore, Calvin C. and John Williamson. "The Universal Fear of Death and the Cultural Response" on Internet.
[2] Ibid

significance of life is threatened by death. Standardized death rites help give meaning to life and death.

People in some cultures fear to talk of death, lest they bring death upon themselves. Extreme measures are taken to follow customs surrounding death lest bad consequences follow. The corpse may be preserved by one means or another in the hope of survival.

In many cultures the fear of death is tied to their fear of the ancestral spirits. Meticulous care is taken to appease the dead lest they strike the living with ill fortune. Intentional efforts are made to demonstrate grief over the person's death lest he or she be accused of causing the death.

Death is not merely a transition to the unseen world of the ancestors; death is an enemy, greatly feared and resented. People feel helpless and hopeless in the face of death. The sense of loss is increased because the dead do not return in human bodies. Their ghosts may return, but ghosts do not show affection or sympathy. Death is a monster that strikes down family members. As the ancient Greek philosopher once said, "Death is the most terrible of all things; for it is the end."

Egyptians

In Egypt, a funeral cult developed in order to provide the needs for the dead king in the after-life. Such items as clothes, food and even servants were buried with the king. Providing for the dead king was essential for the well-being of the nation and progress of the world. The process of gaining everlasting life for the king became the great work of the Egyptians.

Even the ordinary Egyptians observed ceremonies meant to ensure the safe passage of their loved one to the other world. Magical spells were pronounced in order to protect the ghost from harm in his wanderings. Offerings were given to the spirits of the dead who resided in the tombs.

Muslims

Islam, like all other religions except biblical Christianity, teaches that good works are the means of entering paradise after death. Muslim theology, called the *'Tawhid,'* informs a Muslim what he must believe. The Law, known as the *'Shari'a,'* prescribes the rules and regulations which the faithful Muslim must perform. These regulations are burdensome and oppressive, covering every aspect of one's life. On the basis of one's faithfulness in keeping the *sharia* regulations, a Muslim can only *hope* to enter Paradise. But no Muslim can know this with any certainty.

In a religious study of three nations, they found that "Muslims had the highest fear of death."[3] Muslims believe in a demanding and vindictive Allah who punishes wrongdoing. They are less likely to believe in a forgiving God. The eternal destiny and hope of salvation in paradise for all Muslims are known only to Allah and are under his divine control. Muslims have no assurance whatsoever of obtaining their salvation. They have no control over their final destiny, even though Islam teaches that people may hope to be saved by works, provided they are covered by the mercy of Allah on Judgement Day. Nothing in this life can assure them of paradise. Most Muslims can expect to enter the fire at least temporarily. Uncertainty about one's future destiny naturally leads to fear.

Despite Islamic claims, many Muslims fear death. One young man confessed his fears on the internet:

> For the past 3 months, I have been deeply troubled; I am suffering from anxiety and fear of death. Although I know it is inevitable and one cannot escape it, somehow I am not able to overcome it. What exactly troubles me is the moment of dying. Is there any way or any surah or du'aa' to recite in order to overcome the pangs and fear of death?

Hindus

Whereas Muslims believe in life after death, either in paradise or hell, the Hindus believe in reincarnation, being reborn again and again into a new station of life. Depending on what he has done in this life, a human can be re-born as another human being, either as an upper caste if he lived a good life or an out-cast if he lived a bad life; or worse, he or she may be born as an animal or even a plant. What determines the nature of one's reincarnation is *karma* (meaning 'deeds' or 'works'). One's future existence is determined by the thoughts, words and deeds in this life.

Though Hinduism claims that no one should fear death, many Hindus do. Knowing that one has had bad thoughts and deeds, and has left undone many responsibilities in life, this results in "spiritual suffering." Not knowing what your *karma* will lead to in your reincarnation brings fear.

---

[3] Ellis, L., Wahab, E. & Ratnasingan, M. (2012). "Religiosity and fear of death: a three-nation comparison." *Mental Health, Religion & Culture*. On Internet

Buddhists

Buddhism includes many sects and parties that differ in their doctrines and practices, but they are extremely pessimistic, believing life is full of suffering and dissatisfaction. Buddhism, an offspring of Hinduism, embraces the basic beliefs common to Hinduism, namely, reincarnation and *karma*. Gautama became the Buddha ("the enlightened one") after years of meditation when he "discovered" that the cause of suffering in life is *desire*. Through the cessation of *desire*, he believed, all suffering will cease. The path to this detachment of self (emptying oneself of *desire)* is through an eightfold path with right views, desires, speech, conduct, mode of livelihood and right effort. The Buddha offered no help, but only instruction to show the way. Buddhism is a "do-it-yourself religion.

Buddhists teach that there is no "self" to preserve after death. What passes on to the next life through reincarnation is an impersonal consciousness laden with *karma*. The living experience a continual dying, a constant changing from one mode to another. They teach that physical death is not dreadful, but only the beliefs and imaginations of death bring fear. Advocates of Buddhism believe that this teaching alleviates the fear of physical death.

Despite the teachings of Buddhism, many Buddhists fear death. One's destiny is tied up with *karma,* the sum total of deeds done in this life. *Karma* determines whether a person is reincarnated as a plant, an animal, an outcast or as an upper class Brahmin of the priestly class. Buddhist monks and nuns, steeped in the doctrine of "no self," exhibit great fear of self-annihilation. A study was made of Buddhists with a surprising discovery that was contrary to the official views. Despite the official teaching, they found that "Buddhist monks and nuns – those who were steeped in these religious doctrines day in and day out – exhibited significantly more fear of self-annihilation than Americans or Indians."[4]

Chinese

Fear of death is evident in Chinese culture. The Chinese word for the number, 4, sounds very much like *death*. It is therefore no coincidence that the number, 4, is considered unlucky among the Chinese and other Asians. Any digital number with "4" is avoided, such as 4, 14, 24, or 42. Mentioning *four* in the presence of a sick person must be avoided under all circumstances. Military aircraft and ships avoid the number 4 in any digital

---

[4] Web site: *Is there Life after Death,* a Program Sponsored by John Templeton Foundation http: //www.slate.com/bigideas/is-there-life-after-death/essays-and-opinions/buddhism-and-the-loss-of-self

form. Apartment complexes often omit floors 40-49, moving instead from 39 to 50. April 4 (the fourth month of the year) is considered especially unlucky.

Westerners

In the West the fear of death is muted. Though present, it is unspoken. A study was made in America why only a few people choose to invest in annuities that guarantee a steady stream of income during retirement. The insurance company concluded that a large number of people avoid saving for old age with annuities because they don't want to think of their death.[5]

Americans have sanitized death and seek to minimize its impact. People are not exposed to the realities of dead bodies. Instead, they employ professionals to embalm the body, dress the dead in their best attire, and use cosmetics to give the corpse an appearance of life while lying in their silk-lined, guilded coffin. During the graveside service, the casket is never lowered in the presence of those grieving. Americans are shielded from the harsh realities of death. "Cemetaries" are now called "Memorial Parks." In Europe cremation is more common and gravesite services are rare.

Even materialists, who reject all belief in God and spiritual realities, have a muted fear of death because in their thinking death is simply the gateway to an endless state of nothingness. What then is the meaning of life? Innate within every human being is the need to find significance and purpose in life. Death terminates any hope of finding significance and meaning in life.

"The right to die" has become a movement in several western countries, legalizing assisted suicide. In Oregon, U.S.A., the State sanctions physician-assisted suicide when the person is terminally ill. The purpose is to ensure that the dying person "does not lose control of his/her dying process." The thinking is that fear of death would be "overcome and controlled" by the option of suicide."[6]

Following is a nameless westerner who expressed his thoughts of death on the internet:

> *Fear of nothingness after death. No more influence on the mortal world. Fear of nothing after life. Who you are or were is lost forever.*

---

[5] Web site: *Fear of Death Keeps People Away from Annuities* - Annuityfyi.com www.annuityfyi.com.
[6] Sok K. Lee. "East Asian Attitudes Toward Death – A Search for the Ways to Help East Asian Elderly Dying in Contemporary America." *The Permanente Journal* 2009 Summer: 13(3): 55-60. On Internet.

Fear of checking out permanently. Gone and taken back by the earth. Fear that the moment you die, there will be no more thought, no more ideas or opinions. Oblivion, or not even that. No soul to linger on or go to heaven or hell. All good or not so good deeds are for nothing. Fear to just cease existing... Agreeing with the top answer... No more time, thought or influence... Just nihil and it scares the crap out of me too... Funny thing though like after falling, once it happens the fear becomes irrelevant.

CONCLUSION

Whether you live in the East or the West, North or South; whether you live in Europe or Asia, fear of sickness and death is pervasive. It is not always prominent or visible, but it is present to some extent nevertheless. It does not depend on the teachings of the philosophy or religion one adheres to. Fear of sickness and death seems to be built in human nature.

What are the beliefs and feelings about death in Africa that cause fear? The following chapter describes their fears at greater length.

2

AFRICAN TRADITIONS
THAT CAUSE FEAR

As we have seen in the last chapter, all human beings have a tendency to fear sickness and death. Their reasons vary – facing an unknown future, losing personal loved ones and friends in this life, sensing guilt over life's failures, feeling the futility and emptiness of life or uncertainty about future. Generally, their fear of death is *not* associated with evil spirits or mystical powers.

However, for Africans, the source of fear arises not only from human nature, but also from their worldview. For the African, reality includes the physical world and the spiritual world, both being interconnected and affecting each other.

According to African traditional belief, many spirits have been created as spirits and dwell most anywhere: in remote, unpopulated areas of the bush, forest, rivers and mountains; in objects of nature such as trees, rivers or mammoth objects of nature. They may dwell in an animal which approaches a village with people. Since their identity is unknown, they are greatly feared because they can bring untold harm.

Many Africans also believe in ancestral spirits, sometimes called the "living-dead" because they are dead physically, but retain a living relationship with their family. The living know them by name and interact with them. Once the "living-dead" cease to be remembered by name after four or five generations, they became nameless spirits, but continue to interact with the living, mostly with terrifying effects. They are potential sources of sickness and death.

Furthermore, the mystical powers that reside in this world can affect the wholeness and vitality of the living. The reality of harm that can be felt and experienced through curses, black magic, sorcery, witches and witchcraft, are frightening. Although contemporary Africans may understand the physical causes of diseases, they believe that the root origins of sickness and death are caused by intelligent beings, either those in the spirit world or those in this world who utilize mystical powers.

DEATH AND THE SPIRIT WORLD

Nature of Human Beings

Africans throughout the continent believe in a Supreme Being who created the world, including human beings. Approximately, 2,000 creation myths have been recorded in Africa. Africans have understood innately that this vast universe with living creatures never popped out of nothing; neither did the universe exist in eternity past. Traditionally, Africans have never believed in spontaneous generation of life over millions of years and the evolution of the human species. The universe, including the earth, was created by an intelligent and all-powerful creator God.

Africans have always believed that human beings are more than physical bodies. There is a spiritual part of mankind that lives on after the body dies and decays. Some communities taught that a person has both a body and a life-principle or a vital-force. For example, the word for "spirit" in Kikamba comes from the verb meaning "to breathe." The Kamba in East Africa describe death by saying, "his breath is gone."

Other communities like the Ga in West Africa believe in two souls. Thus a human being is composed of three parts. The personality can leave the body during dreams. The soul after death is either reborn into the family or moves to the spirit world as an invisible ghost.

Whatever the individual beliefs may be, Africans uniformly believed that a human being has a spirit in addition to the material body. Most Africans believed that after death the spirit continues to interact with the living, though this belief is not found in every community.

Meaning of Death

Death in African traditional belief does not end one's existence but is a mere transition into another form of life. The dead move from the world of the living to the world of the spirits. The Kamba in Kenya, for example, use the following expressions to convey the idea of death: "going home," "being summoned," "being called,", and "following the company of one's grandfather."

For the Igbo of Nigeria death is necessary for the living to join their ancestors and be venerated as an ancestral spirit. Without death the number of "living-dead" cannot increase. After death the ancestral spirits take time to adjust to their new status as living ghosts. Though death is a necessary part of the cycle of life, death is not welcomed.

Though death means that a person no longer has a body, it does not mean a total separation from the family. In the thinking of the traditional African, the spirit of the deceased continues to interact with the living, both helping and punishing them. But the relationship between the living and their "living-dead" is not peaceful. The ancestral spirits do not normally show affection or sympathy to their living family.

Even though death is a necessary transition to the spirit world, death is feared and resented. It is a cruel monster that snatches a loved one away. People feel helpless and hopeless in the face of death. Like the Tiriki of Kenya and people throughout the world, no African wants to die.

In order to restore the social balance after the departure of a family member, cleansing and purification rites are often performed in order to remove any uncleanness caused by death. Medicines are used to strengthen and protect the living so that they can adapt to life without the departed loved one.

Causes of Death

With rare exceptions, death is never explained in Africa only by natural causes. Though they may understand the natural cause (for example, death through the bite of a venomous snake), the African still asks the question, "*Why* did that snake attack him?" They believe a personal agent is behind death, perhaps a vengeful ancestral spirit who has not been properly remembered and honoured, or perhaps an unforgiving person who used witchcraft to inflict vengeance. The Mandari of Sudan say death is caused ultimately by God, though lesser causes are found as well.

Though God may be acknowledged in some communities as the primary cause of sickness and death, the most common explanation is witchcraft or angry ancestral spirits.

Because death never happens for natural reasons alone, the living must visit the diviner to learn who caused the death. This frequently leads to retaliation. If death is caused by a curse, the diviner enables the afflicted to return the favour by pronouncing a curse on the offender. Thus family feuds with curses may continue generation after generation.

Diviners are also needed after death in order to restore social relationships. Death upsets the balance of life and requires correction. For this reason the Diviner plays a prominent role in prescribing rituals and sacrifices.

Day of Death

Upon the first announcement of death in certain cultures, the women of the household often engage in loud wailing. Family and neighbours gather to join the household women in wailing, beating calabashes, dancing and drumming. Often this natural mourning is exaggerated and magnified in wild despair in order to avoid suspicion of being involved in the cause of death.

The amount of mourning depended on the status of the departed. Funeral rites were seldom observed for a child because the child had never achieved status or power in the culture. An unmarried person was not considered fully human and therefore not mourned greatly. They were not buried in their homestead. Marriage in African cultures is essential. Moreover, marriage without children diminishes the cultural importance of the married couple. The most powerful individuals in this life have elaborate funeral rites and are mourned for longer periods of time.

The reason Africans gave most attention to the death of the old and influential men was to placate the departed so that he would not molest them or cause further sickness and death. Those with great authority in this life were greatly feared in death. The socially inferior, such as children and unmarried, were less of a threat to prosperity and peace of the community.

While mourning takes place, the corpse is prepared for burial or disposal. Customs varied as to what should be done with the body. Traditions must be followed in order to avert any retaliation from the dead. Hence various taboos were observed.

Life after Death

Beliefs of the after-life vary. The Becwana of South Africa believe the spirits live underground where their bodies are buried. The old men are buried under the cattle pen so that they can hear the tramping of the cattle which they loved.

Others believed the "living-dead" ascend to the sky and live somewhere above the earth. But wherever they live, the ancestral spirits are commonly associated with the place of burial and their former abode.

The world of the spirits is often thought to be much like the world in which the living dwell. Boys herd the goats and sheep, women hoe their gardens and men delight in their cattle. Villagers gather for their evening talk, the drums beat and the dances follow. However, many like the Chagga of Tanzania say that the spirit world is inferior to the world of the living for their main food consists of ants, insects and flies. The one major difference is that the "living-dead" never marry.

The status of the "living-dead" is much the same as it was in their former lives. The powerful men retain their authority and can affect the lives of their families still living. Great care must be taken to show the departed ancestors due respect and honour lest they become offended and begin attacking with sickness, disease, famine and death.

In the belief of many Africans, the ancestral spirits serve as guardians of family traditions. They ensure that traditions are kept by all succeeding generations. If anyone breaks these customs, the ancestral spirits will punish the erring person or persons by bringing drought, sickness, or death. Therefore, they are greatly feared. Customs cannot change. Innovations and modernity are banned.

Any failure to keep the traditions and grant the ancestral spirits their due honour, will result in misfortune. This has retarded the development of traditionally bound African cultures which are tethered to the mandates of the ancestral spirits who demand that traditions be maintained.

During this period the "living-dead" must be remembered by name with offerings such as pouring out of libations. Failure to do this will bring blight and pestilence, sickness and death from these ancestors.

The powerful intermediary in African villages is commonly called in English the "witchdoctor" in some communities, although no suitable title has been agreed upon, and each community has its own nomenclature. Though highly respected, he is also greatly feared. He possesses mystical power and knowledge as the medium who deals with the unseen spirits.

Though the "witchdoctor" is generally viewed positively, in many African communities it is believed that he uses the same powers as a witch and can attack people like a witch. Therefore, he is both respected and feared. He is the focal figure of authority in the traditional African community and serves as a diviner, prophet, healer and counsellor.

When consulting with the "witchdoctor," he prescribes the treatment for illnesses and designates the remedy for appeasing the displeasure of the spirits. Because sickness and death are never explained only by natural causes, but by malevolent spirits or neighbouring enemies, the "witchdoctor" is consulted whenever problems arise. Suspicions and fears lurk. He divines to learn the cause of illness. The danger of offending the ancestral spirits compounds the fear of sickness and death.

FEAR OF MYSTICAL POWERS

Belief in mystical powers filled the psychic atmosphere of African traditional communities. This life-force is pregnant in everything from humans to animals, from trees to rocks. Everything that transpires in life, whether good or evil, can be attributed to this vital-energy or mystical power. Specialists with inherited or purchased powers are required to unleash these powers for good or bad.

African communities varied greatly in these beliefs. Following are some examples of mystical powers among numerous Africans, though other Africans may not share the exact same belief.

Curses

Curses in Africa have great potency and foment panic. When an African curses another, this arouses extreme fear because it is believed that the curse is empowered by the mystical power pervading the universe. The curse becomes effective by virtue of the life-force indwelling that person. The power of the curse depends on the status of the one who curses. The more aged and influential the person who utters the curse, the more powerful will be its effect. A husband cursing his wife has the same powerful effect as that of a father cursing his children.

Evil Eye

Certain individuals have inherited an "evil eye," usually identified as one with blood-shot (red) eyes. This person may not intend to do harm, but the power is naturally within the person. A mere stare at someone can cause sickness or death unintentionally. Therefore, mothers shield their babies from the gaze of those with an evil eye, or they cover the baby's face with fat which allegedly neutralizes the effect.

Evil Tongue

Some people have an "evil tongue" that can be detected when the tip of tongue has certain black marks. This person, like the one with an "evil eye," has innate powers which are inherited, passed down generation after generation. Without intending harm, he or she may inflict great injury just by speaking. Compliments are particularly dangerous for the mystical power will reverse the compliment and turn it into a form of curse.

Witch

A witch is by definition someone who has innate powers to effect harm on others and can be activated without the use of any material apparatus or "medicines." Witches are simply evil by nature. Though men may become witches, most are female. Witches are known by their appearance. They may have red, squinting eyes which look down to the earth when talking. Their faces may be ugly or the body disfigured. Because the practice of witches is anti-social, they are feared. Any kind of misfortune is blamed on them. They practice their craft under the cover of darkness. People utilize their powers when they desire to take revenge on an enemy who has done them harm.

Sorcerer

English terminology used to describe African traditional practitioners can be very inexact. Sorcerers are more common than witches, though in popular English terminology their craft is spoken of as witchcraft. Generally, a sorcerer is one who, in contrast to the witch, uses "medicines" of various kinds, such as herbs, roots, bark, insects, skins, bones, leaves and animal horns with incantations to injure others. But primarily, sorcerers use poisons to target persons with deadly consequences. In some cases, poison is used exclusively by the sorcerer. But the poison only achieves its potency to kill if the sorcerer uses incantations and rituals to strengthen its powers.

Black Magic

In many ways a sorcerer is a "black magician," that is, a specialist who engages in nefarious acts. Black magic is the opposite of white magic (terms used by indigenous populations). Whereas, white magic is used for "good" purposes, such as passing a school exam, causing it to rain, or protecting one from harm by an amulet worn on the body, black magic is used only to harm another. The mystical power of black magic is found in the prevalence of vital-force found in nature and utilized by a specialist trained in these skills.

Diviner

A diviner (or "witchdoctor") is a medium who consults with the spirits of the dead and uses mystical powers to thwart the ill-workings of the witches and sorcerers. In contrast to the witch and sorcerer who are anti-social and work under the cover of darkness, a diviner works during the day and is considered a "friend" of the community, albeit, "a feared friend." In certain African cultures, a "diviner" has many specialties, whereas in other cultures, those individual specialties are practiced by a range of different "diviners."

CONCLUSION

Beliefs and traditions among African peoples vary considerably. However, for the most part, fear is common in African traditional communities whenever trouble may strike. This is due to the prevailing worldview. Ancestral spirits may seek revenge because they have been neglected or because the living have broken a taboo and failed to follow the customs of the ancestors. Unknown spirits lurk in the bush, forests, along streams and rivers and in the mountains. Jealousies abound in African villages which lead to acts of retaliation, revenge, vengeance. Witchcraft is a frightening reality.

In brief, fear grips the African. The living use mystical powers to harm others, and the ancestral spirits exact revenge and discipline.

Should a Christian be subject to the same kind of fear as the unbelieving African? When accidents or sickness strike, should this lead Christians inevitably to fear?

How can the Gospel of Jesus Christ deliver a believer from this fear of African traditional reality? Read on to find the answer through the Scripture.

3

Receiving God's Gracious Gift of Salvation

Many Christians do not understand salvation, even though they claim to be saved. Part of the solution for overcoming fear of death is to understand how great is the salvation which Jesus Christ offers, and having assurance that they are truly saved from the consequences of sin. Becoming a child of God is a gracious gift of God's love. Through God's grace we belong to him forever. "Nothing can separate us from the love of God in Christ Jesus." Trusting in God's keeping power, we are protected from all evil.

WHY DO WE NEED TO BE SAVED?

Everyone who has failed to receive God's gracious gift of salvation in this life has every reason to fear death. Death is the consequence of sin as the Scriptures teach, *"For the wages of sin is death."* The MESSAGE paraphrases Romans 6:23 more graphically: *"Work hard for sin your whole life, and your pension is death."* Sin has consequences.

The Bible teaches, *"...it is appointed for men to die once and after this comes judgement"* (NASB). Or as the MESSAGE translates Hebrews 9:27, *"Everyone has to die once, then face the consequences."*

Unless we are alive at Jesus' Second Advent, all human beings, without exception, experience physical death because "all have sinned." But "in Christ" believers are made alive spiritually (Eph 2:4-6) and are "saved" from the second death and eternal condemnation (Ro 8:1). Their penalty for sin has been paid by Christ.

How did Sin Enter the World?

Numerous African communities have varied accounts of a lost paradise. The Ashanti and Akan picture God living in heaven. In the past he lived so close that people could touch him. When an old woman began pounding her grain by using a mortar and long pestle, she accidentally jabbed him and irritated him. This jabbing eventually led to God moving further up into the heavens. The Mende say that separation from God occurred when people bothered him by asking too many questions. Others say that smoke from grass fires annoyed God so he moved away. The Lugbara say that in the past people and God were in direct contact because of man's ability to climb a ladder to the heavens. But eventually that ladder broke and men fell to the ground.

The fascinating truth is this. Although these African explanations for God's separation from humans may seem trivial, they bear witness of a distant memory of a lost paradise with God being close to men and women. Africans believe something has happened that caused God to separate from humans, whatever it was, although this knowledge has been distorted and even suppressed.

As a result, Africans traditionally believe in the creator God, but One that is distantly removed from people today. Yes, in times of crisis they can call upon God for help. But in their daily lives, as long as life carries on as normal, God's presence is not needed. Africans have no solution to their dilemma.

The inspired Word of God, however, provides a more sober account of man's separation, and it provides a solution. The God of creation has graciously provided a remedy for this lost paradise.

We read in Genesis that when God formed this earth and filled it with a vast range of creatures, he said repeatedly, *"It was good."* On the sixth day God created Adam and Eve in his image. They were given authority to exercise dominion over the earth as vice-regents. At the conclusion of the sixth day of creation we read, *"God saw all that he had made and it was very good"* (Ge 1:31). This world was created without sin. Adam and Eve were *"very good"* in God's sight.

But then tragedy struck! Sin entered this world through temptation by Satan, and the yielding to temptation by Adam and Eve (Ge 3:1-7). Satan first planted seeds of doubt in the minds of Adam and Eve: *"Did God really say, 'You must not eat fruit from the tree that is in the middle of the garden?'"*

Satan then contradicted God's warning, *"You will not surely die."* He compounded this lie with a further lie and the lure of exalting human ambition, sensuality and selfishness above faith and obedience to God, saying: *"God knows that when you eat of it your eyes will be opened, and you will be like God, knowing good and evil"* (Ge 3:5).

This has been the tactic of the devil throughout history. Seeds of doubt concerning the trustworthiness of God's Word will inevitably lead to self-centred choices. This exalts self and usurps the sovereign rule of God. Sin makes men and women autonomous agents above God's authority.

Adam and Eve were created innocent and pure with the ability to choose obedience to God or disobedience. This is what we call "free will." Adam and Eve had the ability, the free will, to obey or disobey when God created them.

But everything changed after their fall from grace. As Paul taught, *"...sin entered the world through one man, and death through sin, and in this way death came to all men, because all sinned...*" (Ro 5:12). Through Adam the human race has been born with a sinful nature, generation after generation, and alienated from the favour of God.

What is Sin?

To answer this question we must first consider the Law of God. The Bible says, "*I would not have known what sin was except through the law*" (Ro 7:7).

Why did God give the Law? In order to bring men and women to Christ, he gave the Law so that they might learn God's holy standard of right conduct. The Ten Commandments express God's righteous standard. Jewish rabbis count a total of 613 commandments in the Old Testament.

Of these Jesus said the greatest commandment was: "*Love the Lord your God with all your heart...;*" and the second greatest, "*Love your neighbour as yourself*" (Mt 22:34-40). Loving God summarizes the first four of the Ten Commandments, and loving your neighbour summarizes the final six.

The commandments of God are not a set of arbitrary rules imposed on men and women. The Law reflects the character of God himself. Because God is righteous, just, truthful, loving, kind and good, God requires his creatures, who are made in his image, to be righteous, just, truthful, loving, kind and good. The commandments are "holy, righteous and good" because God is holy righteous and good.

The problem is that since sin entered the world through the Fall of Adam and Eve, no human being keeps God's Law perfectly. In fact, no one is able to keep the whole law because of the sinful nature inherited from Adam. Many people think that they live a good life – "I've never murdered anyone," "I've been faithful to my wife," or "I take care of my family."

But they have never considered carefully what God requires. You may not have murdered anyone physically, but Jesus says, "Anyone who is angry with his brother" has committed murder in his heart. You may not have committed adultery in the flesh, but Jesus said, "Anyone who looks at a woman lustfully has already committed adultery with her in his heart" (Mt 5:21-30).   God's standard of righteousness begins with the heart, and the Bible says, "*The heart is more deceitful than all else. And is desperately sick [wicked]; Who can understand it*" (Jer 17:9 *NASB*).

Even if someone were able to keep much of God's Law, the Bible declares, "*...whoever keeps the whole law and yet stumbles at just one point is guilty of breaking all of it*" (Jas 2:10). Therefore, no one is innocent!

This leaves every man, woman and child in a desperate condition. It leaves them exactly where God intended them to be. The Law was never given to save people if only they would obey the Law, for no one can obey God's law perfectly. As we have seen before, "*I would not have known what sin was except through the law*" (Ro 7:7).

So what is sin? The Bible uses several different words to describe the horrible nature of sin.

1) *Sin is **missing the mark** – not keeping God's holy Law.* The most common word for sin in the original languages of the Bible means "*missing the mark*" (1 Jn 3:4). This word is used in the literal sense of a marksman missing the target (Jdg 20:16). Sin is the failure to "hit the target" set forth in the Word of God, failure to keep the commandments found in it.

    Our thoughts, words and deeds, fall short of God's standard. For example, God blesses us daily with food and clothing, family and loved ones, education and jobs – and the list goes on – but we fail to give God thanks. Living our lives with ingratitude, without a thankful, praising heart is a sign that we fall short of God's demand.

    We may love our neighbours sometimes or somewhat, but we fall short of loving them as we love ourselves; and we surely don't love our enemies. We may love God to some extent, but we fail to love him by God's standard – absolutely, with all of our hearts, and with all of our souls and with all of our minds. So we continually fall short of God's commandments – we miss the mark laid out by God.

    But sin is not merely a falling short of God's will by *missing the mark*. We willfully choose to resist the will of God.

2) *Sin is **rebellion against God***. This Greek word can refer to rebellion against the king. Several words are used with this meaning (Isa 1:2; Eze 2:3; Dt 21:18; Ro 1:30; 2 Ti 3:2). Sin is not a mere failure to hit the mark: it is open rebellion against God's command.

    When Adam and Eve sinned, they willfully chose to rebel against God. They chose their own way rather than submitting to God's expressed command. Autonomy is the great sin of the human race. Men and women, children and youth choose to follow their own desires rather than God's. They set themselves up as kings, answerable to no one but themselves. They turn their backs on the King of kings. Rebellion is heinous in God's eyes and can only lead to a grave penalty.

3) *Sin is **transgression of God's Law***. Literally, transgression is "to cross over." Morally, it refers to going beyond an established limit. For example, when God made a covenant with Israel at Mt. Sinai, they

were required to keep his commandments. That is, they were not to transgress, or "cross over" the covenant boundaries (Dt 17:2,3).

When Israel made the golden calf at Mt. Sinai, they *transgressed,* that is, *they crossed over* the boundary lines set by God in the covenant.

Idolatry is not only bowing down to wood and stone idols. Anything that replaces our supreme devotion and allegiance to God is idolatry. It may be allegiance to ancestors, spirits or divinities. In our times this can be money, women, status, sports, family or any other thing that takes the preeminent allegiance in our lives.

4) *Sin is **irreligion or impiety**.* The Greek word meaning, "not to worship," or "not to show reverence" is used for sin (2 Ti 2:16). Sin is the failure to worship, honour, and love God as he deserves.

Impiety includes failure to worship God in spirit and in truth; neglecting devotion to God with prayer and meditation on God's Word; disregarding God, or living as though God were not very important.

Sin, therefore, is not merely making a mistake or forgetting to do the right thing, or doing something that displeases society. Traditionally, Africans believed that wrongdoing was essentially an offense against society, such as breaking a taboo, or disregarding age-old traditions. According to Scripture sin is against God. It is transgression of his Law.

When David was caught in his adultery with Bathsheba and the murder of her husband, Uriah, he made no excuses but confessed, "*Against YOU, YOU ONLY have I sinned and done what is evil in your sight...*" (Ps 51:4).

What are the Consequences of Sin?

The Lord God is gracious in all his ways because by nature he is good. He lavished on Adam and Eve magnanimous gifts. In the beautiful Garden of Eden, which God had planted for them, he offered the first man and woman a generous array of food: "*You are free to eat from any tree in the garden.*" But he also tested them, saying: "*but you must not eat from the tree of the knowledge of good and evil, for when you eat of it **you will surely die**"* (Ge 2:16-17).

When Adam and Eve defied God, they paid the consequence: they died, just as God had said, and with them, the whole human race in their loins died!

Death is the consequence of sin and death has many forms.

(1) *Spiritual death* transpired immediately when Adam and Eve sinned. They were separated from all fellowship and communion with God. No

sooner than judgement was pronounced on Adam and Eve, we read, "*So the Lord God banished [Adam] from the Garden of Eden*". Moreover, God placed "*cherubim and a flaming sword flashing back and forth to guard the way to the tree of life*" (Ge 3:24). The Lord God no longer walked with them in the Garden; he no longer was their friend who communed with them. Fellowship was broken!

Spiritual death was much more than the literal banishment from the Garden. Sin sank its tentacles deep into the depth of the human soul, corrupting every facet of their personality: their intellect, will and emotions. The whole human race became "dead in transgressions and sins" (Eph 2:1).

Their thinking became futile. They became "*darkened in their understanding and separated from the life of God because of the ignorance that is in them...*" (Eph 4:16-17). Humans may be hugely intelligent, capable of sending men to the moon and exploring outer space. But intelligence is not wisdom. "*Although they claimed to be wise, they became fools,*" by worshipping and serving the creature instead of the Creator (Ro 1:21).

Their will became enslaved to sinful desires, constantly antagonistic to the will of God. "*God gave them over in the sinful desires of their hearts to sexual impurity for the degrading of their bodies with one another*" (Ro 1:24). The "old self" is "*corrupted by its deceitful desires*" (Eph 4:22).

Their emotions became unstable, ranging from simmering anger to lustful temptations, from greed to jealousy. The emotional component of the fallen human race is marked by "*bitterness, rage and anger, brawling and slander, along with every form of malice*" (Eph 4:31).

Because of spiritual death personalities are saturated with sin, producing all the pain and suffering found in our world today. Drunken fathers lead to violence in the home, neglected and abused wives and children, poverty, lack of fees for schooling – a legacy passed on from one generation to another. The toll of sin on society is staggering, including violence, revenge, curses, greed, jealousy, and every kind of evil. Listen to the summation of sin and its consequences in the words of Paul:

> *They have become filled with every kind of wickedness, evil, greed and depravity. They are full of envy, murder, strife, deceit and malice. They are gossips, slanderers, God-haters, insolent, arrogant and boastful; they invent ways of doing evil; they disobey their parents; they are senseless, faithless, heartless, and ruthless. Although they know God's righteous decree that those who do such things deserve death, they not only continue to do these very things but also approve of those who practice them* (Ro 1:28-32).

(2) **Physical death** is what is obvious to everyone. Because everyone has inherited Adam's sinful nature, everyone gets sick and eventually experiences physical death, the separation of the body from the soul. As the Bible teaches, *"The wages of sin is death"* (Ro 6:23). Disease which leads to physical death is minor compared to what follows physical death.

(3) **Eternal Death** or the Second Death follows physical death and is irreversible. *"...man is destined to die once, and after that to face judgement"* (Heb 9:27). Before the judgement of the "Great White Throne" at the end of the age, *"The dead will be judged according to what they had done...If anyone's name was not found written in the book of life, he was thrown in to the lake of fire"* which is *"the second death"* (Rev 20:11-15).

The consequences of rebelling against God, falling short of keeping God's Law perfectly, and neglecting God in worship, is serious beyond measure. The wise person will fear God and submit to his will by placing their trust in Jesus Christ who paid the penalty for their sin on the cross.

How are we Tempted to Sin?

People are tempted today in ways similar to the temptation of Adam and Eve.

> *When the woman saw that the fruit of the tree was*
> *good for food*
> *and pleasing to the eye,*
> *and also desirable for gaining wisdom,*
> *she took some and ate it.*
> *She also gave some to her husband, who was with her, and he ate it*
> (Ge 3:6).

Our own desires have priority over God's perfect will.
As the apostle John wrote:

> *Do not love or cherish the world or the things that are in the world.*
> *If anyone loves the world, love for the Father is not in him.*
> *For all that is in the world,*
> *the lust of the flesh [craving for sensual greatification],*
> *and the lust of the eyes [greedy longings of the mind],*
> *and the pride of life [assurance in one's own resources*
> *or in the stability of earthly things] –*
> *these do not come from the Father but are from the world [itself]*
> (1 Jn 2:15, 16 Amplified).

You will notice that the three enticements of Eve found in Genesis 3 are the same kinds of temptations that come today from "the world."

Genesis 3:6	**1 John 2:15, 16**
"good for food"	"desires of the flesh" (*ESV*)
	"all that panders to the appetites"(*NEB*)
	[This includes gluttony, drunkenness, laziness and sexual immorality]
"pleasing to the eye"	"desires of the eye" (ESV)
	"all that entices the eye" (*NEB*)
	[This includes covetousness and all kinds of envy]
"desirable for gaining wisdom"	"pride in possessions" (*ESV*)
	"all the glamour of its life" (*NEB*)
	"boastful pride of life" (*NASB*)
	[This includes pride in all sorts of things and boasting]

Is Everyone a Sinner?

The one major difference between Eve and human beings today is this: before her disobedience, Eve had the ability to love and obey God; she had the ability to resist temptation and hold fast to God's will. But today men and women are born in sin and no longer have the free will to obey God. By nature they are sinners. Their only free will is the freedom to act according to their fallen, sinful nature. As a fish is free to swim in water (and not fly in the air); and as a bird is free to fly in the air (and not swim under water); so men and women are free to chose whatever their sinful nature desires (and not free to love and obey God perfectly). There are no exceptions, for the Bible teaches, *"All have sinned and fall short of the glory of God"* (Ro 3:23). The Bible teaches:

> *There is no one righteous, not even one;*
> *there is no one who understands, no one who seeks God.*
> *All have turned away, they have together become worthless;*
> *there is no one who does good, not even one* (Ro 3:10-13).

This does not mean that human beings are as bad as they could be. This would be "absolute depravity." They still reflect a smudged, corrupted image of God. A few generations after Cain killed his bother, his descendants created musical instruments and learned how to forge tools from bronze and iron (Ge 4:21f). We find much "goodness" in men and women because mankind is still born in the image of God. Sinners can be honest, kind, generous, helpful and forgiving.

But all these "virtues" are corrupted so that they are not performed out of pure love for God, but with selfish, self-centred reasons. When Adam had children, we read that Adam "had a son in his own likeness, in his own image (Genesis 5:3). In the same way, we all have children "in our own likeness."

HOW ARE WE SAVED?

What is the solution for our sin problem? How can we escape eternal death which is God's judgement for our sins? We have no escape apart from God's grace.

The word, "Gospel," means Good News. For all who are mindful of their hopelessly sinful condition, the grace of God is indeed Good News. The Gospel does not demand and command. Instead, it offers forgiveness freely as a gift.

Unfortunately, many Christians do not understand this. They believe that salvation requires perfect obedience to God's Law in order to be saved. The Good News is that God has provided what we need to be saved by his grace.

No one can receive God's gracious offer of salvation until he or she understands that he or she is a sinner, and under God's judgement. Sorrow for sin and repentance must precede salvation.

Vocabulary Expressing Salvation

Scripture uses different words to describe the many aspects of salvation. Like a finely cut diamond, salvation has multiple facets. There are different ways of describing what takes place when a person becomes a Christian

(1) **"Salvation"** – This word means "deliverance." Used literally, people are *saved* or *delivered* from danger, distress, bondage or adversaries. Spiritually, it refers to being rescued or *saved from the penalty of sin* which is eternal death – eternal separation from God. The Philippian jailor cried out, *"What must I do to be saved?"* Paul replied, *"Believe on the Lord Jesus, and you will be saved..."* (Ac 16:30-31). "Salvation embraces all that is included in God's gracious gift to his people.

(2) **"Regeneration"** – Regeneration is a *re-creation*; in other words, being *born again*. Salvation is not turning over a new leaf or starting over again after making serious blunders. Salvation is not through self effort to live a better life. Regeneration is an act of God in bringing new life to a person. Salvation is the new birth. Jesus shocked Nicodemus, the religious Pharisee,

when saying, *"I tell you the truth, no one can see the kingdom of God unless he is born again"* (Jn 3:3).

Jesus makes it clear that this new birth does not come about through human effort. He goes on to say, *"The wind blows wherever it pleases, you hear its sound, but you cannot tell where it comes from or where it is going. So it is with everyone born of the Spirit"* (Jn 3:8). God's Spirit moves like the wind – unseen, uncontrollable and mysteriously.

The Apostle John affirms that the children of God are *"born, not of blood nor of the will of the flesh nor of the will of man, but of God"* (Jn 1:13). This makes it clear that no one is born again because of his physical birth into a "Christian" home, or because of his ethnic descent from a Christian tradition, or because of any human effort. The New Birth is God's sovereign work of grace, giving new life to those who were "dead in sin" (Eph 2:1).

(3) **"Conversion"** – Like every aspect of salvation, conversion is by grace and grace alone. Conversion means "a complete change," *a turning around*, a dramatic transformation, and includes two aspects: repentance and faith.

<u>Repentance</u> takes place by God's convicting grace when a person, who is called by God, recognizes that he or she has sinned against God and with a contrite and broken heart repents with sorrow for sin committed. In effect he turns away from his sin.

<u>Faith</u> is the second step in conversion by turning to Christ and accepting Jesus as Saviour and Lord.

(4) **"Redemption"** – This word refers to *"the payment of a ransom."* Israel was first in bondage in Egypt, and the Jews were later captives in Babylon. In both cases the Bible says that Israel was "redeemed" from slavery (Dt 7:8).

Spiritually, we were on bondage under the law, unable to free ourselves from the penalty of disobedience. As we read in Galatians, *"Christ redeemed us [paid a ransom] from the curse of the law by becoming a curse for us – for it is written, 'Cursed is everyone who is hanged on a tree...'"* (Gal 3:13).

(5) **"Reconciliation"** – This word refers to "a change of attitude or relationship." It is used literally of enemies or estranged parties being brought together and reconciled, such as Jews and Gentiles being reconciled, brought together, as we read in Ephesians 2:13-16.

Spiritually, our sins alienated us from God whose anger and displeasure for our sin separated us from God. Through faith in Christ's death we are reconciled to God. *"Once you were alienated from God and were enemies in your minds because of your evil behavior. But now he has reconciled you by*

Christ's physical body through death to present you holy in his sight, without blemish and free from accusation..." (Col 1:21, 22).

(6) **"Justification"** – This word means "to pronounce, accept, and treat as just." It is a word referring to an action taken in a court of law wherein an accused person is pronounced "just" and "innocent." This pronouncement changes the legal position of the accused. No longer under the verdict of "guilty," he is pronounced innocent and just and is treated as if he has always kept the law. The Scriptures make clear that people are *justified by faith alone* (Ro 3:22-24).

(7) **Adoption"** – The legal adoption of a child was not common in Africa. In the Roman world the upper classes frequently did adopt a child for the purpose of providing an heir. When the adopted child reached a certain age a public ceremony was conducted in which the adoptive father announced, "He is my son, and he is the heir to my inheritance."

Before believing in Christ, Satan was our father (Mt 13:38; 1 Jn 3:10). But the Bible says, *"...you have received the Spirit of adoption as sons! (Ro 8:15 ESV).* Paul further teaches:

> *But when the fullness of time had come, God sent forth his Son, born of woman, born under the law, to redeem those who were under the law, so that <u>we might receive adoption as sons</u>. And because you are sons, God has sent the Spirit of his Son into our hearts, crying, 'Abba!' Father!' So you are no longer a slave, but a son, and if a son, then an heir through God (Gal 4:4-7 ESV).*

Through the blood of Christ, God redeemed the elect who were enslaved to sin with the devil as their father, and adopted them as sons and daughters into the family of God. This makes every believer an heir of Christ's riches.

What then does the Bible teach concerning salvation? How are we saved?

Salvation is Through Faith in Jesus Christ

Early in the Gospel of John he wrote, *"Just as Moses lifted up the snake in the desert, so the Son of Man must be lifted up, that <u>everyone who believes in him may not perish but have eternal life</u>. For God so loved the world that he gave his one and only Son, that <u>whoever believes in him</u> shall not perish but have eternal life"* (Jn 3:15, 16).

At the end of the Gospel of John, the apostle gave his reason for writing the Gospel: *"that you may <u>believe that Jesus is the Christ</u>, the Son of God, and that <u>by believing you may have life in his name</u>"* (Jn 20:31).

When Peter preached to Cornelius, he concluded by saying, "*All the prophets testify about him [Jesus] that <u>everyone who believes in him receives forgiveness of sins through his name</u>*" (Ac 10:43).

When the jailor in Philippi cried out to Paul, "*What must I do to be saved?*" Paul responded, "<u>*Believe in the Lord Jesus,*</u> *and you will be saved*" (Ac 16:30-31).

How are we saved? Scripture is clear. Salvation is through faith in Jesus Christ who paid the penalty for our sin when he died on the cross in our place.

When the apostle Peter preached to the Jews on Pentecost, to those who had participated in the death of Christ, the Holy Spirit brought great conviction on them and they asked, "*Brothers, what shall we do?*" He replied, "<u>*Repent and be baptized,*</u> *every one of you, in the name of Jesus Christ for the forgiveness of sins*" (Ac 2:38).

Repentance always accompanies faith in Christ. We repent of our sins and turn to Christ in prayer with faith, trusting Jesus to save us.

Scriptures clearly teach that baptism is not a requirement for salvation. Jesus assured the dying thief on his cross that because of his faith, he would be with Christ in Paradise, though he was never baptized (Lk 23:42-43).

But baptism is an outward sign of what has taken place in a believer – dying to sin and rising to a new life in Christ, represented by immersion in water baptism (Ro 6:3-4). Baptism is commanded of all believers who trust in Christ for salvation. In the New Testament baptism followed soon after conversion.

Salvation is by Grace Alone

Apart from the Christian Gospel, every religion in the world teaches that you must *do something* to enter some form of paradise after death. You need to live a good life, keep the commandments, go to church or perform the rituals and ceremonies prescribed by your religion. This is true of Islam, Hinduism, Buddhism and every other belief or unbelief. This is even true of many who claim to be Christian. Whatever people believe about "salvation" or the afterlife, the requirement is good works to please God and merit forgiveness of sins.

The necessity of good works to earn salvation seems like common sense. Try asking most people this imaginary question: "If you die and an angel asks you, 'Why should I let you into heaven?' what would be your answer?" Most people would say, "I've lived a good life, I took care of my family, I have never killed anyone, I never stole." One of the richest men in the world, owning billions of U.S. dollars which he is giving away to charity, recently claimed that when he dies, God will not even interview him, but will usher him straight into heaven! He did so much good! Good works should entitle good people to live forever in heaven.

This innate human belief, that we must do something to earn salvation, crept into the Christian Church during the medieval ages. The Church taught that salvation is by grace *plus* deeds of merit. After one confesses his sins to a priest, he must then perform deeds of satisfaction in the sacrament of penance by recitation of prayers, good deeds, fasting or almsgiving. Salvation in effect is a joint effort by God and man, something which must be gained and maintained by good works.

Martin Luther was upset by the Church selling indulgences. The Pope had offered forgiveness of sins for those in purgatory if a Christian paid money to the Church, a practice called "indulgences." Among his famous 95 theses, posted on the Wittenberg Castle Church door, Luther protested against those who "preach only human doctrines who say that as soon as the money clinks into the money chest, the soul flies out of purgatory." The notion that sin would be forgiven if money were given to the church is contrary to the teaching of Scripture. Papal indulgences issued by the Roman Pontiff cannot wash away sins. "It is vain," Luther contended, "to trust in salvation by indulgence letters, even though...the pope were to offer his soul as security."

Even today, in churches where the Good News of Jesus Christ is preached, many believers think that their salvation depends on what they do; and if they fail to do certain things, they will lose their salvation.

But the Bible teaches the very opposite. We cannot merit our salvation or pay for the forgiveness of our sins. Paul makes this very clear.

But God, rich in mercy, for the great love he bore us,
brought us to life with Christ even when we were dead in our sins;
it is by his grace you are saved.
And in union with Christ Jesus he raised us up and
enthroned us with him in the heavenly realms,
so that he might display in the ages to come
how immense are the resources of his grace,
and how great his kindness to us in Christ Jesus.
For it is by his grace you are saved, through trusting him;
it is not your own doing.
It is God's gift, not a reward for work done.
There is nothing for anyone to boast of.
For we are God's handiwork, created in Christ Jesus
to devote ourselves to the good deeds for which God has designed us
(Eph 2:1-10 NEB).

We are saved by grace alone. Grace is God's blessing bestowed on undeserving human beings. Grace is a gift. It is unmerited favour. The Scripture quoted above states categorically that *"it is by grace you are saved, through trusting him; it is not your own doing. It is God's gift, not a reward for work done."*

Salvation, however, is neither free nor cheap. We cannot pay for our salvation because we are "dead in our sins." What we cannot do, God did. In love God himself graciously paid for our salvation. God had no obligation to save us from the penalty of our sins. He would have remained just and righteous if he had paid out our "wages," namely, eternal death. But for reasons known only to God, and out of a deep love for his chosen ones, he made provision for our salvation by giving his only Son whom he loved to bear our sins in his own body and be punished with death in our place.

Paul clearly explains the way of salvation in Romans 3:20-28.

(1) *For by the works of the law no human being will be justified in his sight,*
since through the law comes knowledge of sin.
(2) *But now the righteousness of God has been manifested apart from the law, although the Law and the Prophets bear witness to it –*
the righteousness of God through faith in Jesus Christ for all who believe.
(3) *For there is no distinction:*
for all have sinned and fall short of the glory of God,
and are justified by his grace as a gift,
(4) through the redemption that is in Christ Jesus,
whom God put forward as a propitiation by his blood,
to be received by faith.
This was to show God's righteousness,
because in his divine forbearance he passed over former sins.
It was to show his righteousness at the present time,
(5) *so that he might be just and the justifier of the one who has faith in Jesus. Then what becomes of boasting? It is excluded.*
By what kind of law? By a law of works? No, but by the law of faith.
For we hold that one is justified by faith apart from the works of the law

The above Scripture teaches the great truths about our salvation which we discuss in the order enumerated by the numbers above.

(1) No one can ever be declared righteous (justified) before God by keeping the Law of God. The purpose for the Law was never to make it possible for sinners to be saved. The Law was given so that sinners would

understand that they are sinners and are unable to please God by keeping the Law perfectly.

(2) Instead of trying to become righteous by keeping God's Law (an impossibility), a different kind of righteousness has been revealed, one that comes from God as a gift. This righteousness was revealed in the Old Testament through the prophets, although its provision awaited the perfect sacrifice of Christ's death.

(3) There is no distinction between Jews and Gentiles, between the religious and irreligious, between those who seem to be good people and those who are outwardly wicked. All are sinners and none can be declared righteous before God – justified – apart from God's grace.

(4) This gift of grace (being declared righteous before God – that is, being "justified") comes at a price which God paid. God gave Jesus to die on the cross in our place. He redeemed us by paying the penalty for our sin so that the wrath of God against us might be appeased. By "propitiation" the Scripture means "appeasement." Through the blood of Christ shed on behalf of sinners, God's wrath was pacified.

(5) The cross represents not only God's love but his justice. God <u>could not</u> have remained a just God if he had forgiven our sins without the penalty for our sins being paid. Christ's death shows us two things: the extent of his love (*"For God so loved the world that he gave us his only Son..."*), and the awesome holiness and righteousness of God which requires payment for our sin before forgiveness was offered.

Salvation is by Faith Alone

The rallying cry of the Protestant Reformers was not only "Grace Alone," but "Faith Alone." People are saved, justified, redeemed, and reconciled to God by faith alone, apart from any contribution that they can offer. This is clearly taught in the New Testament writings of the Apostle Paul.

We have quoted Ephesians 2 above from *The New English Bible. The MESSAGE* renders these verses graphically in a free paraphrase which shows that faith and trust in Christ's saving death on the cross is all we can do to be saved:

Saving us is all his idea, and all his work.
<u>All we do is trust him enough to let him do it</u>.
<u>It's God's gift from start to finish!</u>
We don't play the major role. If we did, we'd probably go around bragging that we'd done the whole thing!
No, we neither make nor save ourselves (Eph 2:6-9 The MESSAGE).

But doesn't James contradict Paul? Martin Luther thought so, but a more careful reflection on these verses shows otherwise. These are the controversial pronouncements of James:

> *What good is it, my brothers, if a man claims to have faith*
> *but has no deeds? <u>Can such faith save him?</u>*
> *Suppose a brother or sister is without clothes and daily food.*
> *If one of you says to him, 'Go, I wish you well; keep warm and well fed,'*
> *but does nothing about his physical needs, what good is it?*
> *In the same way, <u>faith by itself, if it is not accompanied by action, is dead</u>"*
> (Ja 2:14-17).

The solution to this seeming contradiction is simple. There is more than one kind of faith. James asked the man who claimed to have faith, but failed to show love by helping the needy, "Can *such faith* save him?" We could translate it by saying, "Can *that kind of faith* save him?" The answer is a resounding "No!"

The first reference to "faith" has no article in the Greek. The second reference to "faith" (*"Can **such faith** save him?"*) has an article which has the effect of pointing to the word, "faith." It has a demonstrative force, pointing out the individual identity of faith. "Can that particular kind of faith save him?" The answer is "No!"

True saving faith works. Though no one is saved by faith **plus** works, we are saved by faith **for** good works (Eph 2:9-10). Justification is by grace alone and through faith alone. But the kind of faith that saves a person also transforms him and her into a new person in Christ Jesus. The new heart in Christ is immediate, but growing into the likeness of Christ is a process that gradually occurs in the life of a believer. Everyone who is saved manifests a changed life with a love for God and the desire to please God by obeying him. The fruit of obedience to God is evidence of saving faith. The Scriptures are clear on this:

> *Therefore, if any person is (ingrafted) in Christ, the Messiah,*
> *he [or she] is (a new creature altogether,) a new creation;*
> *the old (previous moral and spiritual condition) has passed away.*
> *Behold, the fresh and new has come (2 Co 5:17 Amplified).*

Faith can be mere intellectual assent, agreeing with a proposition. A person can believe the Gospel intellectually without being saved because it is a nominal profession of faith, a profession in name only. Saving faith is *trusting in* Jesus Christ to be your Saviour in response to God's gracious offer of salvation.

The two kinds of faith can be illustrated by the daring tight-rope walk across the Niagara Falls, stretching along the border of Canada and the U.S.A., by Jean-Fancois Gravelet on June 30, 1859. Great crowds gathered to watch this feat. Before the awe-struck eyes of thousands of spectators, he walked on a tight-rope hundreds of feet above the roaring, churning waters of Niagara Falls. Did the swarms of people *believe* he could do this? Of course they *believed* for he had demonstrated before their eyes his ability!

But when he offered to carry someone across on his back, no one *believed* in him and entrusted their lives to him. They assented, they believed in their heads, they agreed in their thinking that he could do it, but they would not *entrust* their lives to him. There is a major difference between mentally believing that Jesus died for them and actually trusting (resting on) him to save them.

Salvation by faith in Jesus Christ alone means that a person believes he or she is lost, under God's wrath and judgement because of sin against God. That person also believes that Jesus Christ died for his or her sins and will grant salvation when that person repents and trusts Christ to save by *entrusting* their eternal destiny to him.

Frequently, the New Testament uses the preposition *in* or *on* after the word, "believe," to emphasize a restful reliance on Jesus Christ who died for us. You depend on Christ to forgive your sins and save you from damnation. You not only believe *that* Jesus died to save you (mental assent), you actually *believe in* Jesus, resting *on* Jesus. As the Scriptures teach, *"Believe in the Lord Jesus Christ, and you shall be saved"* (Ac 16:31) *"...whoever believes in him shall not perish but have everlasting life"* (Jn 3:16).

Salvation is through Christ Alone

The focus of the Protestant Reformation was on salvation which had been so distorted by the extra-biblical traditions which the Church added over the centuries, like purgatory, a doctrine taught nowhere in the Bible. Salvation, according to the Scriptures, is by "grace alone," through "faith alone," and in "Christ alone." Christ alone saves from sin.

It is no accident of history that the Cross became the symbol of Christianity because the death of Christ is the focal point of Scriptures. Immediately after the sin of Adam and Eve, God made for them garments of skin by shedding the blood of an animal. This was a type for the clothing of righteousness which God would provide all those who trust in Christ – and that garment was made possible through the death of Jesus, "the Lamb of God."

At the same time the Lord promised a Saviour (the "offspring" or "seed" of the woman) who would defeat Satan. The Lord spoke to the serpent [Satan], saying: *"And I will put enmity between you [the serpent, alias Satan] and the woman and between your offspring [seed] and hers; he will crush your head, and you will strike his heel"* (Ge 3:15). Though Satan would strike a non-lethal blow on the heel of the offspring (alluding to the painful death of Christ), the promised seed of the woman would deliver a death blow to Satan by crushing his head.

Throughout the Old Testament, sacrifice became the central act of Israel's worship. Sin offerings, guilt offerings and burnt offerings were offered "to make atonement." The atoning sacrifices made satisfaction or amends for injury. God's glory and honour have been injured by our disrespectful disobedience. Atonement was necessary to make amends.

Every Jewish male brought a lamb as an offering. By laying his hand on the lamb, he symbolically transferred his sin and guilt onto the animal. Then the lamb was slain and its blood sprinkled on the altar to make atonement. We read in Leviticus 17:22, *"For the life of a creature is in the blood, and I have given it to you to make atonement for yourselves on the altar; it is the blood that makes atonement for one's life."* Offering the lamb as a sacrifice was also an expression of a repentant heart for sins committed, and a demonstration of trust in God for his forgiveness.

It is no accident that many people groups throughout the world, including Africans, have traditionally offered bloody sacrifices of goats, chickens and occasionally some cattle in order to appease the offended and gain favour. Remember that all peoples today have descended from Noah and one of his three son: Shem, Ham and Japheth. Before the flood and afterwards Noah offered animal sacrifices and this practice was no doubt handed down generation by generation.

In Hebrews 10 we read the New Testament interpretation of the Old Covenent sacrifices in light of the coming of Christ.

> *The law is only a shadow of the good things that are coming –*
> *not the realities themselves.*
> *For this reason it can never, by the same sacrifices*
> *repeated endlessly year after year,*
> *make perfect those who draw near to worship...*
> *But those sacrifices are an annual reminder of the sins, because*
> *it is impossible for the blood of bulls and goats to take away sins...*
> *we have been made holy through*
> *the sacrifice of the body of Jesus Christ once for all* (Heb 10:1-10).

Christ's whole life pointed to the cross. When Jesus first appeared at the Jordan River, John the Baptist cried out, *"Look, the Lamb of God, who takes away the sin of the world"* (Jn 1:9). Though Jesus did teach and heal during his three years of ministry, and though Jesus did demonstrate his deity and messianic identity through many signs, the primary purpose of his incarnation was his sacrificial death. Half of John's Gospel is devoted to the last week of Jesus' life. Of the 33 years which Jesus lived, more than one-third of the Synoptic Gospels covers the last week of his ministry.

The last book of the Bible records the worship of the Lamb as they sing: *"...with your blood you purchased men for God from every tribe and language and people and nation"* (Rev 5:9f). Towards the end of Revelation "the wedding supper of the Lamb" takes place (Rev 19:9).

Christ's sacrifice was offered once for all times. Before giving up his spirit on the cross he cried out, *"It is finished."* Atonement had been completely provided. Christ had finished his work on the cross. Christ and his atonement alone, made on the cross, has dealt fully and finally with the sin problem. No works of satisfaction or penance, no indulgences or a further sacrifice of Christ in the Mass are needed. Christ fulfilled all the requirements of a righteous God. As we read in Hebrews 9:24-28, nothing can be added to what Christ accomplished on the cross.

But as it is, <u>he has appeared once for all at the end of the ages to put away sin by the sacrifice of himself.</u>
And just as it is appointed for man to die once,
and after that comes judgement,
so <u>Christ, having been offered once to bear the sins of many,</u>
will appear a second time,
not to deal with sin but to save those who are eagerly waiting for him

HOW CAN WE BE ASSURED
OF OUR SALVATION?

A survey was made of students who entered a Kenyan Bible College in the 1980s. None of them had ever heard a sermon on the assurance of salvation. Only after their instruction in biblical theology did they gain a personal assurance that they were born of God and forever children of God.

There was one exception, one student who had assurance of his salvation. He had been taught by his pastor the biblical basis of salvation by God's grace.

The tragedy is, according to reports, many pastors are afraid to preach on assurance of salvation because they fear that this would lead their parishioners to sin. Many pastors fear that if Christians would know that they cannot lose their salvation, this would lead to spiritual carelessness and tolerance of sin. As a result these pastors preach constantly against sin, but say little of the grace of God that saves from sin.

Certain churches embrace Arminian theology which teaches that a Christian can lose his salvation. Other churches who hold to salvation by grace alone, through faith alone, in Christ alone, have poorly taught pastors and elders so that Christians hear little of the biblical basis for salvation. Because God sovereignly chose his people for himself, and graciously adopted them as his beloved children, we can be assured of our salvation. He who chose us will keep us for his own.

Following is the biblical basis for assurance of salvation.

Feelings come and feelings go. But feelings are not reliable indicators that we are saved. Feelings are not the basis for assurance of salvation. Feelings must be based on objective evidence that does not change. We find this objective evidence within God's Word. Following is the biblical teaching that should be pondered, believed, and embraced by every believer.

(1) Assurance of Salvation Offered by God

The apostle John wrote his Gospel so *"that you may believe that Jesus is the Christ, the Son of God, and that by believing you may have life in his name"* (Jn 20:31). He wrote his first letter to those *"who believe in the name of the Son of God so that you may know that you have eternal life* (1 Jn 5:11f).

From these verses we learn that God desires us to KNOW THAT WE HAVE ETERNAL LIFE. God wants us to have assurance of our salvation.

Some churches teach that it is arrogance or pride to say that you are certainly saved. Others teach that no one can have full assurance of salvation because you may lose it when you sin.

But the whole purpose of the apostle John writing his first letter is to help Christians be assured of their salvation.

(2) Confidence in the Trustworthiness of God's Promises

Our assurance of salvation is based on God's promises. Since God is true and cannot lie, *we should have confidence in the trustworthiness of his Word*.

Adam and Eve lost favour with God by doubting God's Word. Today we find forgiveness from God by trusting (believing) in God's promise.

- The Bible teaches, *"For God so loved the world that he gave his one and only Son, that whoever believes in him [Jesus Christ] shall not perish but have everlasting life"* (Jn 3:16).

- The Bible teaches, "<u>Whoever believes in the Son has eternal life</u>, but whoever rejects the Son will not see life, for God's wrath remains on him" (Jn 3:36).
- The Bible teaches, "He [Jesus] came to his own [the Jewish people] and his own received him not. But to <u>all who did receive him, who believed in his name, he gave the right to become children of God</u>..." (Jn 1:11-12 ESV).
- The Bible teaches, "<u>That if you confess with your mouth, 'Jesus is Lord,' and believe in your heart that God raised him from the dead, you will be saved</u>. For it is with your heart that you believe and are justified, and it is with your mouth that you confess and are saved...<u>Everyone who calls on the name of the Lord shall be saved</u>" (Ro 10:9-10, 13).

The truth that we learn from these verses is that *believing with your heart* results in salvation. Saying a prayer that does not come from the heart does not save.

Secondly, we need to confess with our mouth our faith in Christ. Private faith is not the biblical norm. Baptism naturally follows conversion because it is a public testimony before others of your commitment to Christ.

Thirdly, trusting in Jesus to save you must include confession of his lordship over your life. Whenever Christ saves you, he must become your Lord and Master. "Jesus is Lord of all or he is not Lord at all."

These are just a few of God's promises. The simple question is this: Do you believe what God has promised? Do you trust in Jesus Christ to save you from your sins through his shed blood? If you do, you can rest assured of your eternal salvation. God cannot lie. We are able to rely on what God has promised us in his Word.

(3) Confidence in God's Power to Keep Us

Not only may we have confidence in the trustworthiness of God's Word, we can have confidence in God's power to keep us.

God Saves Completely: When God saves us, he saves us completely. What God starts, he will complete. He does not start the process of salvation and then abandon us to ourselves. We can be confident that God *"who began a good work in you will carry it on to completion until the day of Christ Jesus"* (Php 1:6).

The Bible teaches, *"Therefore <u>he is able to save completely</u> those who come to God through him, because he always lives to intercede for them"* (Heb 7:25).

When the Lord saves us, it is not a partial or temporary salvation; *he saves completely*. As the ESV translates this, "he is able to save to the uttermost" and "at all times."

Further, this total and complete salvation is based not only on Christ's death, but on his continual intercession for us before our heavenly Father. At the present time Christ is seated "at the right hand of God" and is "indeed interceding for us" (Ro 8:34 *ESV*).

God Guards Powerfully: We read in God's Word, *"…I know whom I have believed, and am convinced that <u>he is able to guard</u> what I have entrusted to him for that day"* (2 Ti 1:12).

Not only is Christ able to save completely, *he is able to guard our lives* which we have entrusted to him until that day when he returns.

Anyone who is born again is a child of God whom he guards and protects. There can be no better "guard" or "watchman" than God. He never falls asleep at night like many watchmen do. He is never overcome by robbers who have superior weapons. If God guards what we have committed to him, we can rest assured that our salvation is totally secured.

God Seals Forever: When anyone places their faith in Jesus Christ for their eternal salvation, *God seals them by the Holy Spirit*, guaranteeing their eternal salvation.

Having believed,
<u>*you were marked in him with a seal, the promised Holy Spirit,*</u>
who is <u>a deposit guaranteeing our inheritance</u>
until the redemption of those who are God's possession…
(Eph 1:13-14)

In ancient times a seal was a stamp guaranteeing ownership. When a person believes in Jesus Christ, God the Holy Spirit indwells the person and becomes the guarantee of divine ownership. Furthermore, the inheritance promised to all believers is guaranteed by the seal. We are "sealed for the day of redemption" (Eph 4:30). We have not yet received our full inheritance in Christ. We long for "the redemption of our bodies" when Christ returns and our earthly bodies will be transformed ino his likeness. The Holy Spirit, who indwells every believer, is the seal that <u>guarantees</u> our full and complete salvation.

God's Sheep will Never Perish: The Apostle John provides a deep and abiding assurance that *God keeps his sheep – he knows them, he chose them, and he will forever keep them*.

My sheep listen to my voice; I know them, and they follow me.
I give them eternal life, and <u>they shall never perish;</u>
<u>no one can snatch them out of my hand</u>.
My father, who has given them to me, is greater than all;
no one can snatch them out of my Father's hand (Jn 10:27-30).

Our heavenly Father gave his sheep to Jesus. All genuine believers are Jesus' sheep and they "shall never perish" and no one can snatch them from Christ's hand.

God's Love will Never Leave Us: Nothing can separate us from the love of Christ. Paul exclaims,

"I am convinced that neither death nor life, neither angels nor demons, neither the present nor the future, nor any powers, neither height nor depth, nor anything else in all creation, will be able to separate us from the love of God that is in Christ Jesus our Lord" (Ro 8:38-39).

These concluding verses of Romans 8 are the capstone of what Paul taught in the first eight chapters of this book. Notice the tightly linked chain in 8:28-30. Those whom God **foreknew** with love, he **predestined** to be conformed to the likeness of his Son, and effectually **called** them to faith in Christ. Those very ones were **justified** and will be **glorified.** This is an unbroken chain. Those whom God foreknew with love and predestined are the very ones who will be glorified with none of them lost.

Notice that the verbs are in the past tense ("called," "justified," "glorified"). Those whom God predestined, **he glorified** (past tense). For the Christian, our glorification awaits the future return of Christ. But the future glorification of all believers is so certain that the Bible places this in the past tense. Be assured that all believers will, beyond a doubt, be glorified.

This undivided link-chain ensures that Christ's sheep, those whom God foreknew and gave to Christ, will one day be glorified with Christ in heaven. It is an accomplished fact. Romans 8:35-39 declares explicitly and comprehensively that **nothing** can separate them from God's abiding love – neither sickness nor death; neither curses nor spells; neither black magic, witches nor sorcerers. **NOTHING can separate us from God's loving care!**

(4) Evidence of the New Birth

As mentioned earlier, the Apostle John wrote his first letter to help Christians find assurance that they are God's dear children. This is a wonderful portion of Scripture to meditate on. In this letter we find that a God-fearing life is evidence of the new birth. Notice John's declarations:

"We know that we have come to know him if we obey his commands. The man who says, 'I know him,' but does not do what he commands is a liar, and the truth is not in him...This is how we know we are in him: Whoever claims to live in him must walk as Jesus did" (1 Jn 2:3-6).

"No one who is born of God will continue to sin, because God's seed remains in him; *he cannot go on sinning, because he has been born of God.* This is how we know who the children of God are and who the children of the devil are: *Anyone who does not do what is right is not a child of God; nor is anyone who does not love his brother"* (1 Jn 3:9-10).

"We know that we have passed from death to life, because we love our brothers. Anyone who does not love remains in death...This is how we know what love is: Jesus Christ laid down his life for us. And we ought to lay down our lives for our brothers...Dear children, let us not love with words or tongue but with actions" (1 Jn 3:14f).

In these verses the apostle John is not teaching sinless perfection, for he clearly stated in the same letter, *"If we claim to be without sin, we deceive ourselves and the truth is not in us"* (1 Jn 1:8).

In the Greek language the present tense carries the meaning of "continuous, on-going action." The King James (Authorized Version of the Bible) is technically correct when it says, *"Whoever is born of God doth not commit sin...he cannot sin because he is born of God"* (1 Jn 3:9). But the translation inadvertently carries the wrong connotation. It fails to convey the nuance of the Greek language. John never intended to say that a Christian "does not sin," or that "he cannot sin," but that he does not continue on in a lifestyle of sinning, that he cannot go on continually sinning. A genuine Christian is sorry for his sin. He grieves over his disobedience and confesses his sin. When a person is sorry for sin committed and makes a heartfelt confession and desires to please God, this is evidence of being born again.

What John does teach is exactly what Paul taught: *"...if anyone is in Christ, he is a new creation; the old has gone, the new has come!"* (2 Cor 5:17). Anyone who has been born again is a new and changed person. His lifestyle changes. He loves God, loves God's people, and desires to please God through obedience.

(5) Inner Testimony of the Holy Spirit

Our assurance of salvation is not only through faith which rests on a trustworthy and powerful God to keep us. It not only includes evidence of new life in a believer, wrought by the indwelling presence of the Holy Spirit. Our assurance of salvation includes the inner testimony of the Holy Spirit, a quiet and peaceful confidence in God to save and keep. Some believers may receive instant assurance. Others may struggle and need to grow in their understanding of God's promises before they gain full assurance. But this is what the Scriptures teach.

"*Now it is God who makes both us and you stand firm in Christ. He anointed us, set his seal of ownership on us, and put his Spirit in our hearts as a deposit, guaranteeing what is to come*" (2 Co 1:21-22).

When any person is born again, the Holy Spirit comes to dwell within that person. In fact, Paul says, "*If anyone does not have the Spirit of Christ, he does not belong to Christ*" (Ro 8:9). John teaches, "*We know that we live in him and he in us, because he has given us of his Spirit*" (1 Jn 4:13).

By giving us his Spirit, God seals us for himself. This objective reality means that we belong to God permanently and forever. **No one, not anything** can break that seal by which God is claiming, "You are mine forever." The presence of the Holy Spirit in our lives guarantees our future eternity with God. This objective reality now lays the groundwork for our inner assurance.

The Phillips translation of Paul's teaching in Romans 8:15-17 reads thus:

> *...you have been adopted into the very family circle of God and you can say with a full heart, 'Father, my Father.' The Spirit himself endorses our inward conviction that we really are the children of God. Think what that means. If we are his children we share his treasures, and all that Christ claims as his own will belong to all of us as well! Yes, if we share in his sufferings we shall certainly share in his glory.*

We can know by faith from the Scriptures that we are God's children because of the fruit of the Spirit in our lives. The Holy Spirit "*endorses our inward conviction that we really are the children of God.*" Through the indwelling Holy Spirit we gain a deep and abiding assurance and confidence that we belong to God eternally. What a great gift God has given to us – so great a salvation based on God's grace alone, through faith alone in Christ alone, and we can enjoy a full and abiding assurance that we are his.

Examination of your Life

As wonderful as these assurances are, Paul does caution us to examine our lives. He urged the Corrinthians Christians, "***Examine yourselves** to see whether you are in the faith; test yourselves. Do you not realize that Christ Jesus is in you – unless, of course, you fail the test?*" (2 Co 13:5).

Paul's command to "examine yourselves" cuts two ways. On the one hand, serious Christians may experience doubts of their salvation from time to time. Loss of assurance does not mean the loss of salvation. Assurance of salvation is not necessary for actually possessing salvation. Feelings ebb and flow. If doubts arise, "examine yourselves" in the light of the Scripture and rest assured in God's faithfulness according to his Word. He has all the power to preserve us for himself. God's promises are reliable.

On the other hand, some professing Christians need to examine themselves to know whether their profession of faith has been genuine and whether there is some measure of fruit in their lives to demonstrate that they truly love the Lord and are depending on Christ alone to save them.

Some people respond to an invitation in church, raise their hand or say a prayer of repentance and faith, and assume that they are now born again. If they are saved, the fruit of their salvation will be seen in some measure. Jesus said, *"By their fruit you shall know them."* A regenerate person loves God, loves fellowship with God's people, communes with God in prayer and longs for the pure spiritual milk of God's Word, and is sorry for his sins whenever he or she falls short.

There are professing Christians who claim assurance of salvation, but have no right to be assured. Jesus warned his hearers:

<u>Not everyone who says to me, 'Lord, Lord,'</u>
<u>will enter the kingdom of heaven,</u>
but only he who does the will of my Father in heaven.
Many will say to me on that day, 'Lord, Lord,
did we not prophesy in your name,
and in your name drive out demons and perform many miracles?'
Then I will tell them plainly, I never knew you.
Away from me, you evildoers! (Mt 7:21-23).

Reasons Believers May Doubt their Salvation: Conditions arise that may cause God's children to feel uncertain whether they are truly born again.

- **Neglect of Teaching on the Grace of God**. The Church needs more teaching on the perfections of God – his holiness and righteousness so that they may learn to reverence and fear God. Christians are called to follow in the footsteps of the Lord. We read, *"Be holy because I am holy"* (1 Pe 1:16).

  However, there needs to be a balance between teaching the awesome holiness of God with his righteous standards found in the God's Law, and the mercy and grace of God towards us. Notice the balance in John's writings: *"My little children, I write this to you so <u>that you will not sin. But if anybody does sin,</u> we have one who*

*speaks to the Father in our defense – Jesus Christ, the Righteous
One. He is the he atoning sacrifice for our sin..."* (1 Jn 2:1-2).

Focusing on the holiness of God while neglecting the grace of God
can lead to guilty feelings and loss of salvation. We need to embrace
the grace and loving kindness of our Saviour. We are saved by grace
alone, and by faith alone that brings new life to all believers.

- **Feelings of Guilt May Afflict the Conscience**. If this is guilt for sins
which we have confessed, it is a false guilt. We need to claim God's
promise, believe his Word and rejoice in God's forgiveness. The Bible
teaches, *"If we confess our sins, he is faithful and just to forgive us
our sins and to cleanse us from all unrighteousness"* (1 Jn 1:7).

   But if this is guilt for sins we are still committing, this guilty feeling
is from God. Our conscience can be God's voice which convicts of
sin. Such feelings of guilt should lead to repentance and turning
from disobedience to God.

- **Trials of Various Kinds Can Lead to Doubting God's Love and a Loss
of Assurance**. James reminds us:

> *Consider it pure joy, my brothers,*
> *whenever you face trials of many kinds*
> *because you know that the testing of your faith*
> *develops perseverance. Perseverence must finish its work,*
> *so that you may be mature and complete, not lacking anything*
> (Jas 1:2-4).

God uses various kinds of trial to test our faith and develop within us Christ-
like character that perseveres in loving God despite our afflictions.
Perseverence in Christian faith with fruit bearing is itself evidence of genuine
conversion.

Jesus gave a parable of four kinds of soil, each representing differing
hearts: hardened earth on a path, rocky soil, soil with thorns and good soil
(Mt 13:3-23).

The seed which falls on the hard earth never takes root and never shows
signs of growth. But the seed that falls on rocky soil and on soil with thorns
and thistles begins to germinate and grow. These plants offer hope of a
future harvest. No doubt the farmer is pleased with his prospects. But when
the thorns grow up, they choke the good plants which die. The seed falling
on rocky soil fails to grow deep roots so that when the withering sun beats
down on the plants, they wilt and die.

People may profess faith in Christ and show early promise of becoming
fruitful Christians. But life has many challenges that can undermine faith.

Troubles of many kinds arise. Persecution from family members, the clan and friends may test a Christian's commitment. The many worries and temptations in life may draw people away from Christ so that they pursue worldly ambitions and fall away in unbelief.

The seed that fell on good soil continues to grow (he or she perseveres) and bears fruit. The Bible clearly teaches that those who have placed their faith in Jesus Christ can be assured of their eternal salvation.

Blessed is the Christian who learns to rejoice in hope in the midst of troubles. Blessed is the one who clings to God in faith, despite the problems that beset the Christian.

CONCLUSION

Many Christians fear death because they are not confident that they themselves have been born of the Spirit. They lack assurance, fearing that if they fall sick and die, they may not be with Christ in eternity. These Christians fall prey to temptation. They easily fall back into the traditional customs and depend on witchcraft and appeasement of the spirits to solve their problems. If believers do not understand the basis for his salvation, they may continue to fear sickness and death.

Fundamental to overcoming the fear of sickness and death is a deep understanding of the biblical teaching on salvation and a heartfelt acceptance of what God promises to all his children.

4

MAKING A COMPLETE BREAK WITH MYSTICAL POWERS AND THE ANCESTRAL CULT

Westerners have been deeply influenced by the anti-supernatural approach that was introduced during the Enlightenment. This so-called "age of reason" of the 18th century interpreted all experiences naturally, excluding all supernatural. Even though western evangelicals believe in miracles and the spirit world, their inclination has been to label it superstition whenever they were confronted with the mystical powers of African reality.

Africans know better. They have experienced the powers of darkness. They have lived close to the spirit world and know its reality.

What are these spiritual and mystical powers? How should a Christian deal with them? For this we must turn to the Scriptures.

BIBLICAL TEACHING OF THE SPIRIT WORLD

The worldview of the Scriptures is compatible with many aspects of the African worldview for they embrace a three-fold tier of reality: the physical world where humans live, the spirit world, and the heavenly realm where God dwells. While westerners tend to exclude the middle tier, the realm of the spirit world is both African and biblical.

The Old Testament is a God-centred book. The Creator God is sovereign with infinite power over all creatures. For this reason, the Old Testament is generally silent about spirits. It surely is not preoccupied with demons. This should be a warning to Christians today who are obsessed with evil spirits. To be God-centred is to have such confidence in the sovereignty of God that they need not fear spirits or be engrossed with them. Their focus should be on God and not spirits.

Rebellion of Angelic Beings

According to the Scriptures, God is surrounded by myriads of angelic beings who worship and serve him continually (Isaiah 6; Revelation 4-5). Apparently, at some point a portion of these holy angels rebelled against God, including the chief adversary of God, though not much is said about this. Compare Isaiah 14:12-15 and Ezekiel 28:2.

The chief adversary of God is Satan, also called the devil. The Bible implies that Satan is a demon (Lk 10:17-20). Jude refers to "angels who did not keep their positions of authority but abandoned their home" (Jude 6).   Clearly, at some point in time these beautiful angelic beings whom God created good, rebelled against him and became the evil spirits.

In the Bible these fallen angels are referred to as "demons," "unclean spirits" and "evil spirits" (Dt 32:17; Mk 1:24ff; Ac 19:12ff). These rebellious angels who became "demons" and "evil spirits" are allied with fallen men and women who are part of the kingdom of darkness, ruled over by the prince of the power of the air (Eph 2:2).

Spirit World in the Old Testament

The worship performed by the nations surrounding Israel was forbidden because such worship was idolatrous. It was in fact the worship of demons. For this reason God wanted the nations utterly removed from the land which God had given to Israel. God had redeemed Israel from bondage in Egypt and established a covenant relationship with them at Mt. Sinai.

But in disobedience Israel allowed the nations to live among them so they intermarried and followed the religious practices of their Gentile neighbours.

Reality of the Spirit World: Psalm 106 recounts the history of Israel and narrates how they sacrificed to demons along with the wicked Canaanites.

They did not destroy the peoples as the LORD had commanded them,
but they mingled with the nations and adopted their customs.
They worshiped their idols, which became a snare to them.
*They sacrificed their sons and their daughters to **demons**.*
They shed innocent blood the blood of their sons and daughters,
*whom they sacrificed to the **idols of Canaan**,*
and the land was desecrated by their blood (Ps 106:34-38).

Because the Israelites allowed the demon-worshipping Canaanites to live in the land, they mingled among them, learned their evil customs and began sacrificing their own sons and daughters to the idols of Canaan which the Psalmist calls **demons.** Pagan religions do not worship dumb, lifeless objects, but are worshipping the demons which animate and energize pagan worship. See also Deuteronomy 32:16-17 and 1 Corinthians 10:20.

Reality of Mystical Powers: The Bible recognizes the reality of mystical powers. When the magicians in Pharaoh's court performed miracles similar to those which God performed through Moses, those Egyptian mystical powers were not dismissed as superstition (Ex 7:11,22; 8:7,18,19; 2 Ti 3:8).

They were simply proved inferior to God's power when the magicians were unable to perform other miraculous feats done by Moses. Scripture assumes the reality of demonic forces, even though it teaches their ultimate defeat.

However, not all claims to mystical powers are legitimate according to the Bible. In the book of Acts Bar-Jesus was a magician who held people captive by his persuasive powers. Paul rebuked him, not only saying that he was "a child of the devil," but that he was "full of deceit and trickery" (Ac 13:9). Paul recognized the trickery of many specialists who delve into the occult arts. Africans have likewise recognized the deceitfulness of many diviners.

These mystical powers are not neutral or innocent, but demonic powers, energized by the arch enemy of God. Numerous references are made to them in the Old Testament Pentateuch and Prophets, as well as the New Testament, and they are uniformly condemned.

Spirit World in the New Testament

In contrast to the Old Testament, the Gospels are full of references to spirit possession. The word, "demon," occurs 52 times in the Gospels and only eight times elsewhere in the New Testament.

Scripture does not explain the reason for this sudden explosion of spirit activity. Perhaps it was because the ministry of Jesus made a frontal attack on the kingdom of Satan with his demons, and they reacted defensively as their authority was under threat.

From the Gospels we learn that the demons can influence, control and oppress people; and they oppose the good. Though spirits are not corporeal with physical bodies, they can cause physical things to happen. They are real in every sense of the word though they are invisible to humans.

Though reference to Satan, demons and evil spirits are found less often in the apostolic writings, they are a reality with which the apostles reckoned. During the ministry of Paul and Silas in Philippi, a demon possessed girl followed them and pestered them to the point that Paul, vexed in his spirit, cast out the fortune-telling spirit (Ac 16:16ff). Numerous references are made to "rulers," "authorities," "powers," "thrones" and "world rulers" which we understand as demonic spirits (Ro 8:38ff; Eph 1:20f; 6:11ff).

Hence, from the biblical perspective the spirit world is real, and Christians need to know how to respond to those spirits which have been witnessed and experienced before coming to faith in Christ.

Denunciation of Spiritism and Mystical Powers

The most exhaustive listing of these powers is found in Deuteronomy 18:9-13.

When you enter the land the Lord your God is giving you,
do not learn to imitate the detestable ways of the nations there.
Let no one be found among you
who <u>sacrifices his son or daughter in the fire</u>,
who practices <u>divination</u>,
or <u>sorcery</u>,
<u>interprets omens</u>, engages in <u>witchcraft</u>,
or <u>casts spells</u>,
or who is a <u>medium</u> or <u>spiritist</u>
or who <u>consults the dead</u>.
Anyone who does these things is detestable to the Lord,
and because of these detestable practices
the LORD your God will drive out those nations before you.
You must be blameless before the LORD your God. The nations you will
possess listen to those who practice sorcery or divination. But as for you,
the LORD your God has not permitted you to do so.

The whole premise for these prohibitions is that Israel had a special relationship with the LORD their God. They were a *"people holy to the LORD [their] God, chosen out of all the peoples on the face of the earth to be his people, his treasured possession"* (Dt 7:6). Those nations whom Israel was commanded to dispossess were under the control of Satan. The powers that energized and empowered those forbidden practices were demonic and utterly forbidden.

In the words of the apostle Peter, Christians today are *"a chosen people, a royal priesthood, a holy nation, a people belonging to God"* (1 Pe 2:9). The Church today is the Israel of God and belongs uniquely to Jesus Christ and him alone. Many are offended by these assertions but they come straight from the Word of God. Therefore, Christians dare not have any attachment to the mystical powers experienced in traditional African society.

Divination

Those practices forbidden by God included divination, the attempt to acquire hidden knowledge through supernatural powers. Various means have been used to do this, such as the examination of the liver, interpreting patterns of bones, seeds, or other items thrown on a skin by a specialist, spirit possession, interpreting omens and a multitude of other means.

African specialists display extraordinary powers like foretelling the future and locating a lost item. What could be wrong in seeking help from a diviner who can offer practical help? From the biblical perspective, seeking help from a soothsayer is treasonous for this breaks faith with God. Even if divination is for a "good" purpose and socially acceptable, it must not be utilized by a child of God, for the supernatural powers do not emanate from God, but from evil spirits hostile to the Kingdom of God.

Mediums

Mediums of any kind are explicitly forbidden in the Bible for they bring the living into personal communication with the spirit world of fallen angels. The Old Testament is filled with warnings against those who consult the dead.

> Someone may say to you, 'Let's ask
> the mediums and those who consult the spirits of the dead.
> With their whispering and mutterings, they will tell us what to do.'
> But shouldn't people ask God for guidance?
> Should the living seek guidance from the dead?
> Look to God's instructions and teachings!
> People who contradict his word are completely in the dark.
> They will go from one place to another, weary and hungry.
> And because they are hungry,
> they will rage and curse their king and their God.
> They will look up to heaven and down at the earth,
> but wherever they look,
> there will be trouble and anguish and dark despair.
> They will be thrown into the darkness (Isa 8:19-22 NLT).

Not only are God's people warned against necromancy (speaking to the dead), the mediums themselves were put to death under the Old Covenant. "A man or woman who is a medium or spiritist among you must be put to death. You are to stone them; their blood will be on their own heads" (Lev 20:27).

Sorcery and Witchcraft

All of these evil practices condemned in Scripture have deep roots among the European peoples in their distant past. When Christianity was first introduced to Europeans, the Church struggled to stamp out these practices. In recent decades, with the decline of biblical Christianity in the West, the occult has increased dramatically. The dark side of reality has a grip on those who are not indwelled by the Holy Spirit and prepared for the spiritual battle.

So it should not be a surprise that African Christians also struggle with the whole range of occult practices mentioned in Deuteronomy. Witchcraft includes both the deadly work of witches and the work of those specialists who seek to counteract the witches (the diviners or "witchdoctors"). Anyone who uses drugs, herbs, or any other means to bring about supernatural effects for harming others is totally forbidden.

Not only was Israel forbidden to peer into the future through the means of diviners, they were forbidden to attempt any control of the future. Such activity reflected lack of faith in God and a defiant dependence on the occult.

Therefore, both "white" magic and "black" magic are forbidden. Charms of any kind, which are designed to protect or harm magically, should not be utilized by Christians. Consulting a specialist in the daylight for "good," or in the darkness of night for "evil" is prohibited.

THE CHRISTIAN'S NEW ALLEGIANCE

Conversion involves a turn-around, a 180 degree complete change of direction. Before one has been born again, an unbeliever followed *"the ways of this world and of <u>the ruler of the kingdom of the air, the spirit who is now at work in those who are disobedient</u>." "All of us also lived among them at one time, gratifying the cravings of our sinful nature and following its desires and thoughts"* (Eph 2:2-3).

In mercy God *"rescued us from the dominion of darkness and brought us into the kingdom of the Son he loves"* (Col 1:13). A believer's whole worldview changes from darkness to light, No longer is Satan the master. Jesus Christ becomes both Saviour and Lord.

For those who have been entangled in the works of darkness, they need to make a complete break with the past. Friendships and alliances with those who engaged in witchcraft, sorcery, and mystical powers must be severed.

SPIRITUAL WARFARE

For those Africans who have been converted out of the traditional worldview with intimate experience and knowledge of the spirit world, it is necessary for them to make a clean, public break with those powers that bound them in the past. The second and third generation Christians who have not had personal involvement with mystical powers also need to be well taught in these matters so that they can find deliverance from the snares that entangle so many African Christians.

The Christian is in spiritual conflict with unseen powers (Eph 6:12). Like the traditional African, the Christian is engaged in an encounter with the spirit world of darkness. But unlike the traditional African, Christians have been provided all that is needed to overcome the forces of evil.

Our conquest is based on Christ's accomplished work of redemption on the cross. Christ has already "triumphed over them by the cross," having "disarmed them," making them powerless (Col 2:15). Although the destruction of the devil and his kingdom of darkness has been accomplished in the heavenlies, he and his legions of fallen angels wreak havoc in this world on the human race, blinding and enslaving them.

Satan's chief tactic is deceit and deception. He "disguises himself as an angel of light" (2 Cor 11:14). This effort to deceive can be traced back to the Garden of Eden when he appeared as a serpent and distorted the Word of God. If Satan would appear in his hideous panoply of evil, no one would be attracted to him. Instead, he disguises himself. Theologians believe that he even disguises himself as ancestors in order to attract devotion and homage.

Satan's power is attractive to the natural man who is not indwelled by the Spirit of God. Satan's power is enormous, producing supernatural effects. He comes with *"all power and false signs and wonders, and with all wicked deception for those who are perishing because they refused to love the truth and so be saved"* (2 Th 2:10 ESV). These powers are manifested in the use of magic, witchcraft, sorcery, curses, charms and the like.

Since "it works," people are persuaded. Since it is helpful, many Christians find comfort in it. But the question should be, "Is it from God?" Does God's Word indicate that "it is true"? In order to please the Lord Jesus Christ and find peace and security in this life, serious steps must be taken to make a complete break with all mystical powers and the ancestral cult.

It is therefore necessary that a public renunciation be made with all that has been associated with the occult. The experience of many has demonstrated that the Christian must destroy all objects associated with mystical powers and spiritism. It would appear that the evil spirits attach themselves to those physical objects associated with their activity in the past. The public renunciation of the occult in the presence of other believes and the profession of faith in Jesus Christ should accompany the destruction of all occult objects.

Experience has demonstrated that a new Christian will lapse back into the old traditional practices of African Traditional Religion unless a complete break is made. All ties with the ancestral spirits must be severed. All items of witchcraft must be destroyed. Friendship with those who had contact with the spirit world must be severed.

Those who have been immersed in African realities know full well their power of temptation. A complete break with the past must accompany the profession of faith. Compromise or ambivalence will only lead to defeat and falling back to the old ways.

EXAMPLE OF PUBLIC RENUNCIATION

The Church in Africa has known this for many years. Whenever any African comes to faith in Christ, if he or she has visited a witchdoctor or has in his or her possession objects associated with witchcraft, sorcery or magic, these must be publicly renounced and destroyed.

Under the leadership of the pastor and elders in the Africa Inland Church in Kenya among the Kamba, a Christian service is conducted at the convert's house. Christians join together to witness and support the convert's public testimony of faith and the renunciation of former allegiances. In public the convert gathers all the charms, fetishes and materials associated with the traditional practice of witchcraft, sorcery, white magic, black magic, and the ancestral spirits.

The service includes much singing, claiming the blood of Christ to vanquish the powers of darkness. The pastor or elder delivers a biblical message followed by a personal testimony of faith in Christ by the convert in which he or she renounces all the works of Satan. The pastor and elders help the convert light a fire which burns all the items heaped on a pile. In order to ensure a complete destruction of the paraphernalia, twigs and logs are added to the bon fire. All the time the congregation sings hymns of triumph.

CONCLUSION

Conversion *always* involves a complete change, a turning around and change of allegiance. Every human being is born into the kingdom of darkness. Conversion always includes rescue from the dominion of Satan and the transfer into the Kingdom of God.

Experience has shown, however, that for those who have trafficked in the mystical powers of darkness and have such paraphernalia in their houses, these items must be completely removed from the dwelling and utterly destroyed during a public service of Christian testimony.

In cases where whole communities have been steeped in darkness and under the dominion of Satan, extraordinary steps may need to be taken to ensure that Satan no longer has a foothold in that person's life. A spirit possessed person will need to experience total deliverance from any demon oppression. These evil spirits lurk hidden in people's lives. Their presence is made known only by the new convert's inability to grow strong in the Lord, frequently lapsing back into the old ways of African Traditional Religion.

Overcoming fear of death requires not only a genuine conversion and an understanding of salvation by grace alone; it requires a complete break with everything and everyone that pertains to these mystical powers.

5

TRUSTING IN THE
TRIUMPH OF CHRIST OVER SATAN

Since the early church, numerous symbols have been used for Christianity.
One of the earliest symbols is the fish which is found drawn on the walls of
the Roman catacombs where Christians hid under ground, worshipped and
buried their dead. The Greek word for fish is ιχθυs (*ichthus*).
Christians made an acrostic of this word, consisting of the initial
letter of the following five words in Greek: *Jesus Christ, Son of God, Saviour.*
Jesus, personal name (from Greek), Joshua (from Hebrew), means Saviour.
Christ, (from Greek), Messiah (from Hebrew), means Anointed One.
Son of God, identifies Jesus as God, second person of Trinity.
Saviour, the one who saves us from our sins.
Even today the *ichthus* can be seen posted at numerous sites. The fish
(*ichthus*) shows that the focus of Christianity is on Jesus Christ.

A common symbol found in liturgical churches is the *Chi-Rho*. It
was first inscribed on the walls of the Roman catacombs. The first
two Greek letters for the word, *Christ*, are χ and ρ. Thus the symbol
points to Christ.

However, the most common symbol of Christianity throughout
history is the cross. It is often worn on the body as an ornament and
may be a personal testimony; it is inscribed on tomb stones, planted
on church steeples and placed in prominent positions within the church
sanctuary. Christians even cross themselves, identifying them as Christians.

There is good reason why the cross has become the universal symbol of
the Christian faith. The cross represents the heart of the Gospel of Jesus
Christ, that *"Christ Jesus came into the world to save sinners."* Jesus shed his
blood for our salvation.

The shedding of blood occurred throughout the Old Testament in the
sacrifices offered in the Tabernacle in the wilderness, in the Temple in Shiloh,
in Solomon's Temple, in the second Temple and in the Herodian Temple in
Jesus' day.

It is no accident that most Africans have been offering bloody sacrifices for
generations before the coming of the Gospel, providing a glimpse of the
gospel light. This tradition may have been passed down to them through the
descendants of Ham, son of Noah, or from the Jews who fled Israel and

migrated down the Nile where they made settlements. Unfortunately, the true meaning was lost over time in Africa since the sacrifices are most often offered to the spirits, ancestral spirits and the divinities to appease their wrath.

PURPOSE OF CHRIST'S DEATH

The death of Christ on the cross fulfilled the Old Testament prophecies and accomplished three purposes. Christ's death (1) provided redemption for lost sinners; (2) glorified God; and (3) defeated Satan and his evil spirits.

Redemption of Sinners

The first purpose of Christ's death, providing redemption, has already been discussed. It has been helpful to the author, whenever thinking of the cross, to think of the two cross bars as symbolic of the cross's meaning: The vertical bar (standing upright) represents the uprightness of God, his justice, righteousness and holiness, while the horizontal bar (lying down) represents his love, mercy and grace towards sinners.

Through the cross God was able to (1) justify sinners, and (2) remain righteous in the process by paying the penalty of death himself (Ro 3:26).

The Horizontal Bar of the Cross – symbolically representing God's love: When we think of the cross, we generally think of God's love and mercy shown toward sinners, for the Bible teaches: *"But God demonstrates his love toward us in this: While we were still sinners, Christ died for us"* (Ro 5:8). Salvation of sinners was thereby provided through Christ's death.

The Vertical Bar of the Cross – symbolically signifying God's righteousness – his uprightness: The biblical teaching of Romans 3:26 shows that the significance of the cross goes beyond the love of God. How could a righteous judge declare a sinner innocent (righteous) when in fact he was not? *"The wages of sin is death..."* (Ro 6:23). No judge could be considered fair, honourable and just if he released a guilty person.

By providing his only Son to pay for the penalty of the sinner, God remained just and righteous even while forgiving the sinner who trusts in Christ.

Glorifying God

God, the Creator and Sustainer of the vast universe, is glorious in all his perfections. He is dazzling in his holiness and splendour, amazing in his grace and worthy of all praise, glory and honour.

God has displayed his glory in two creative acts: the creation of the universe and the creation of a people for God through Christ's death.

"The heavens declare the glory of God; the skies proclaim the work of his hands" (Ps 19:1). The splendour of the universe glorifies the infinitely great power and wisdom of the Creator. The revelation of God's glory is "clearly" seen by all peoples, though in their sin they suppress this knowledge (Ro 1:18-20).

But only one aspect of God's glory is seen in creation, his attributes that are reserved for himself and cannot be shared by any other: that God is the almighty, all-knowing, eternal Creator, infinite in all of his perfections.

The cross of Jesus Christ reveals the other aspect of God's glory not made known in creation, namely, his righteousness and his loving kindness, tender mercies and grace. These are divine attributes, possessed by God in perfection, but bestowed to his children in limited measure.

As Jesus approached his impending death, he spoke of it in terms of glorification, saying: *"The hour has come for the Son of Man to be glorified"* (Jn 12:23). The following verse confirms this understanding.

A short time later he repeats the same thought, saying, *"Now is the Son of Man glorified and God is glorified in him. If God is glorified in him, God will glorify the Son in himself, and wll glorify him at once"* (Jn 13:31-32).

How and in what way, we may ask, does the cross glorify God?

First, no greater love can be shown to anyone than a willingness to die for someone else. To die for one's enemies is matchless and divine. When this willing sacrifice is made by the Creator for his rebellious creatures, this is breathtaking. The cross magnifies and glorifies God's love, mercy and grace.

Second, the cross reveals the overwhelming righteousness of God as we have seen. The Judge of all the earth can only do right if penalties for wrongdoing are meted out fairly. God demonstrated his matchless love at the cross, and at the same time, demonstrated his awesome righteousness.

Destruction of Satan and his Minions

When Christ died on the cross, he not only paid for our redemption, but he also triumphed over Satan and utterly destroyed his power and authority over believers. The dark powers of magic, curses, witchcraft and the spirit world have been vanquished in the heavens. But in order for Christians to experience joy and confidence in the face of sickness and death in this world, every believer needs to embrace this truth by faith.

It may be helpful first to consider briefly how these spiritual powers were treated by many of the early missionaries to Africa.

The pioneer Protestant missionaries from U.K. and America in Kenya, for example, were all evangelicals who believed the Scriptures. Without question, they believed in a literal personal devil and the spirit world. They did not share the naturalistic unbelief of liberals who dismissed the accounts in the Gospels as explanations of pre-scientific peoples.

On the other hand, they had grown up in the west where the cultures were highly influenced by the naturalistic worldview of the Enlightenment. They themselves had no experience with overt demonic activity such as demon possession. These Bible believing missionaries believed in the spirit world in theory, but in practice they tended to view the accounts of spirit activity in Africa as superstition. This approach to the traditional African worldview was then passed on to the Africans whom they trained as evangelists and pastors.

On one occasion a fine, godly pastor, whom the author admired, was preaching to his congregation. When he dismissed the workings of the spirits as "superstition," a woman in the congregation stood up and contradicted him in public. She declared before the pastor and the congregation that she knew that these spirits were real and that they could do strange, unusual and frightening things because she had experienced them herself.

One reason why many African Christians have fear of sickness and death may be due to the failure of addressing these issues from Scriptures. This needs to be done in this chapter.

TRIUMPH OF CHRIST OVER SATAN

In this chapter we shall examine carefully the two major Scriptures that teach the triumph of Christ over Satan and his dominion of darkness with its mystical powers and spirit beings.

Christ Broke the Power of the Devil
(1) Because God's children are human beings –
made of flesh and blood – the Son also became flesh and blood.
For only as a human being could he die,
(2) and only by dying could he break the power of the devil,
who had the power of death.
(3) Only in this way could he set free
all who have lived their lives as slaves to the fear of dying.
We also know that the Son did not come to help angels,
he came to help the descendants of Abraham.
(4) Therefore, it was necessary for him to be made in every respect
like us, his brothers and sisters,
so that he could be our merciful and faithful High Priest before God.
Then he could offer a sacrifice
that would take away the sins of the people.
Since he himself has gone through suffering and testing,

he is able to help us when we are being tested
(Heb 2:14-18 *NLT*).

We will seek to expound the above Scripture in the order enumerated by the above numbers.

(1) The first observation from this text is that God's Son was born in a human body with flesh and blood, like the men and women ("children") for whom he came to redeem. He could not die for his people and take on their punishment without being born as a human being. Just as people are born and die, so God's Son was born in order to die. But whereas, men and women die because of their own sin, God's Son died in order to bear penalty for the sins of his people and thus save them from bearing their own penalty.

(2) The second observation is that Christ's death **broke the power of the devil**, *the tempter,* who had brought death into the world through his temptation of Adam and Eve. The Authorized Version (King James) translates this with the word, *"destroy"* – *"through death he might destroy him that had the power of death."*

This surely needs an explanation because the devil does not act like his power has been "broken," much less "destroyed."

First, we must look at the accomplishment of Christ's death from an eternal perspective. The devil's future destruction has been sealed. At the close of this age, *"the devil, who deceived them, [will be] thrown into the lake of burning Sulphur...and will be tormented day and night for ever and ever"* (Rev 20:10). This was made possible by Christ's death.

However, in this age the devil is still active and continues to exercise considerable power over his own people. But the fact is that he has been rendered powerless over believers. His power has been broken. Perhaps *The Message* has best captured the intent of the Scripture: *"By embracing death, taking it into himself, he [Jesus] destroyed the Devil's hold on death."* The devil no longer has a hold on death. He has been rendered powerless.

Satan is a vanquished foe for all believers. Many pioneer missionaries did a disservice when they dismissed spirit activities as "superstition." But some contemporary churches today do an even greater disservice by placing so much emphasis on the devil instead of Jesus Christ. Satan is a defeated foe. He is powerless to molest the believer when the believer relies on Christ, the Victor. Our focus should be on Christ, not on the devil. Meditate on the victory of Christ over death and do not focus on the devil. His hold on death has been destroyed. He has been rendered powerless over God's children.

(3) <u>The third observation</u> is this: Because Satan has been rendered powerless and his power over death has been broken, Christians should no longer fear sickness and death. The children of Adam and Eve have traditionally been living in fear of death, but this has all changed with the death of Christ. God has provided in Christ all that is needed to free believers from the fear of death.

Here is where many believers fall short. Fear and defeat strangle many a believer for any number of reasons: they may be harboring sin in their lives, they may not be nourishing their faith through prayerful meditation on God's Word, or they may not be armed with the spiritual armour of God. The following chapter will explain the biblical teaching on how Christians can and should grow strong in the Lord.

Those in African Traditional Religion have indeed been enslaved. Interviews of African Christian converts tell of the poverty inflicted on the people as the ancestral spirits demanded more and more bloody sacrifices until the Africans had nothing. One woman confessed, "All that I experienced [in her traditional religion] tried to tear my life apart. If it were not for God's powerful hand, I would have died." She went on to say, "ATR made homes to be unhappy and without development. It made women feel inferior because we were regarded as useless things before men. Christianity has made us feel like important human beings in the world."

Faith in Christ brought deliverance from this enslavement. Fear was removed because of their trust in Jesus Christ who triumphed over Satan.

(4) <u>The fourth observation</u> offers encouragement for all who face testings of one kind or another. Jesus Christ, as a full-blooded human being, endured tests and temptations like everyone else, beginning with his temptations in the wilderness, and continuing throughout his life. Therefore, he is able to understand and sympathize with us. He knows what being human is like, for he himself was fully human, but without sin, while also being fully God.

Therefore, Christ has become a compassionate and faithful high priest, not just because he is God, but because he is the God-Man and has endured life as a human being. Jesus saves us not only by his death but also by his life as our great high priest. He is our mediator before God in the present. He is our advocate who pleads our case. We go to him in prayer.

So when we are tempted to fear, we can pray and seek his help. When we fall short of God's perfection, we seek his forgiveness. We can claim the promise that, "If God is for us, who can be against us?"

Christt Disarmed the Spirits

> *(1) And you, who were dead in your trespasses*
> *and the uncircumcision of your flesh,*
> *(2) God made alive together with him,*
> *(3) having forgiven us all our trespasses by*
> *canceling the record of debt that stood against us with its legal demands.*
> *This he set aside, nailing it to the cross.*
> <u>*(4) He disarmed the rulers and authorities*</u>
> <u>*and put them to open shame*</u>
> <u>*by triumphing over them in him*</u>.
> (Col 2:13-15 ESV)

(1) <u>The first observation</u> is that the **Colossians were dead in their trespasses**. They were spiritually dead in their sins before conversion. As uncircumcised Gentiles they are reminded of their former alienation from citizenship in Israel and their morally impure hearts. Uncircumcision did not make Gentiles morally unclean, but it was a symbol of their former fleshly (carnal) immoral state.

Everyone needs to understand and embrace this truth – whether they are Chinese living under the ethical code of Confucious, or Arabians adhering to the Muslim religion, or Latin Americans born in the Roman Catholic Church, or Westerners with a Christian heritage, or Africans following their traditional religion – everyone is born into this world spiritually dead. Dead people cannot help themselves. They cannot save themselves. They cannot breathe life into themselves. Only God can raise the dead, including the spiritually dead.

Cultural pride should never blind believers of their spiritual state in the eyes of God apart from their faith in Jesus Christ. Paul stated the facts boldly:

> *Remember that at that time you were <u>separate from Christ</u>,*
> *excluded from citizenship in Israel and*
> *foreigners to the covenants of the promise,*
> <u>*without hope and without God in the world*</u> (Eph 2:12).

The spiritual state of all unbelievers is "without hope and without God in the world." All people know <u>*about God*</u> because of natural revelation, but they don't <u>*know God*</u> in a personal relationship. They are spiritually dead in their sin, "separated from Christ."

(2) <u>The second observation</u> is that **God gave them the new birth, making them alive in Christ.** Christians are responsible to witness by sharing their faith with others. Christians pray that their witness will bring people to saving

faith in Christ. But it is not possible for any Christian to save unbelievers – to give them new life in Christ. Only God can raise the dead by the Holy Spirit. Jesus makes this very clear.

> *You must be born again.*
> *The wind blows wherever it pleases.*
> *You hear its sound,*
> *but you cannot tell where it comes from or where it is going.*
> *So it is with everyone born of the Spirit...*

> *Yet to all who received him, to those who believed in his name,*
> *he gave the right to become children of God – children born*
> *not of natural descent,*
> *nor of human decision*
> *or a husband's will,*
> *but born of God* (Jn 3:8; 1:12-13).

No one is born again by a human decision or in virtue of being born in a Christian home. The new birth, like the wind that blows beyond our control, happens only when the Spirit of God moves in and grants birth, making them a child of God.

(3) The third observation is that **the record of debt against us is forgiven – canceled – by nailing it to the cross.** Paul here addresses both Jewish and Gentile believers. The legal demands of the Old Testament covenant were given to the Jews at Mount Sinai. The Jews agreed to obey them (Dt 27:14-26). The Gentiles never had the Law of Moses, but they were given a conscience which told them what was right and wrong (Ro 2:12-16). Both Jews and Gentiles failed to keep God's commands and therefore they owe a debt which they cannot pay.

With a figure of speech Paul speaks of this debt being hand-written on a note of obligation. This note is signed by each person, acknowledging that he or she has this debt to pay.

But God in his mercy nailed it to the cross on which Christ paid for our debt. For those who repent and believe, this note of indebtedness is canceled, that is, the handwritten note was rubbed out, wiped off the slate and erased, just as the chalk on a blackboard is erased or pencil marks are erased by a rubber/eraser. This means that the sins of a believer in Christ are forgiven, leaving the believer free of all debt.

The biblical truth found in the three points made above, refer to the first provision made by Christ on the cross: the payment for our redemption. Our sins have been paid for through the blood shed at Calvary.

(4) <u>The fourth observation</u> is that **Christ disarmed the evil spirits and triumphed over them on the cross.** The "rulers and authorities" are the spiritual powers of darkness, as we read in Ephesians 6:12: *"For we do not wrestle against flesh and blood, but against the rulers, against the authorities, against the cosmic powers over this present darkness, against the spiritual forces of evil in the heavenly places"* (Eph 6:12 *ESV*).

On the cross Jesus Christ *disarmed* the evil spirits. This rare Greek word for "disarm" makes the emphatic assertion that the evil spirits have been stripped of their power and authority. Their future damnation has been rendered certain and their present ability to exercise dominion over believers has been stripped away. They are disarmed.

The imagery of a triumphal procession portrayed here is graphic and arresting. Roman armies marched against their enemies throughout the Mediterranean world. Time after time the Roman armies prevailed over their enemies. The triumphant general returned to Rome with his victorious soldiers and their captive enemies. In a great triumphal procession and to the applause of Rome's residents, the generals led the victorious army through the city followed by their humiliated captives.

The Bible speaks of making "a public display" of the captives, literally, "exposing" them to humiliation, having triumphed over them through Christ. The *Message* paraphrases this graphically, *"He stripped all the spiritual tyrants in the universe of their sham authority at the Cross and marched them naked through the streets"* (Col 2:15b The *Message*). This is an accomplished fact. These evil spirits have been "stripped naked," and publicly humiliated under Christ's rule. It is our responsibility to deal with the powers of darkness in this light.

We know that that evil spirits continue to exercise power, but it is limited and circumscribed. The devil does play havoc with those who are not active in faith, with those who have not protected themselves with the armour provided by God (Eph 6:10-18).

But the evil spirits are <u>unable</u> to molest believers who trust in Christ. Paul indicates that we do *wrestle* against these evil powers, but with the armour of God, we can resist and stand. Victory is never in doubt. Believers can "stand firm" and not be defeated.

The apostle John teaches, *"It is the Son of God who keeps him safe, **and** <u>the evil one cannot touch him</u>"* (1 Jn 5:18b *NEB*). God keeps the believer safe and the devil <u>cannot touch him</u>.

John wrote, *"I write to you, young men, because you are strong, and the word of God lives in you, and <u>you have overcome the evil one</u>"* (1 Jn 2:14b). The believer is strong when the Word of God is loved and believed. As a result, a believer overcomes the evil one just as Christ overcame Satan's temptation through the Word of God.

In another letter Paul describes a similar procession of triumph: *"But thank God! He has made us his captives and continues to lead us along in Christ's triumphal procession. Now he uses us to spread the knowledge of Christ everywhere, like a sweet perfume"* (2 Co 2:14 NLT).

Believers, purchased by the blood of Christ, are led in a triumphal procession by the victorious Christ. Through the lives and Christian witness of all believers, the aroma of Christ's victory is spread everywhere. Defeated Christians can only ooze foul smells which can never attract unbelievers to Christ. But believers stand in the triumph of Christ over all spiritual powers of darkness. Through the witness and testimony of victorious Christians, made possible by Christ's victory, we exude the fragrance of Christ. Defeated Christians cannot do that. In Christ we are more than conquerors over the dominion of darkness.

CONCLUSION

The biblical truth is this: Christ has triumphed over Satan and all evil spirits through his death and resurrection, the two key aspects of Christ's victory over sin and death.

This wonderful truth means that the evil spirits have been disarmed and Satan has been rendered powerless and the Christian has a rock solid hope in his own resurrection from the dead.

Many Christians live in ignorance of the hope they have in Christ. They are ignorant of the access they have to the same power that raised Jesus from the dead. They don't understand that God's Spirit dwells in them and can empower them to overcome the powers of darkness and all fears of sickness and death if only they will use the means of grace available to them.

The two responsibilities that Christians have are to **trust** in Christ and **obey** his Word. Unless the believer lays hold of these biblical truths, he or she will remain fearful and defeated.

The keys to victory over sin and fear are discussed in the following chapter.

6

GROWING STRONG
IN THE GRACE OF CHRIST

Joy springs out of pain when a tiny baby is born. Pride and pleasure radiate from the parents. Mom cuddles her little one while Dad gazes with pride and wonder. News travels quickly, and soon the whole village is rejoicing that a new born child has been welcomed into their clan.

But what will their feelings be in another year if the tiny baby remains small and undeveloped? Will those parents and family continue to feel wonder and excitement with a tiny baby one year later?

The birth of children is exciting, but we have every expectation that they should grow. A stunted infant who does not mature into an adult is both abnormal and cause for great concern.

The same is true with the spiritual birth of Christians. The Bible teaches that a new Christian convert is a spiritual baby (1 Pe 2:2). Infancy is the first stage of growing into childhood, followed by adolescence and adulthood when the formerly little infant has fully grown to the point of marrying and having his or her own family. Just as an African passes through various socially accepted stages in life, so a Christian grows.

As important as salvation is, there is much more to the Christian life. Overcoming fear of death should occur when a person is justified by faith and saved from the penalty of sin. By all rights he should have no fear of death. But in order to grow strong in faith one must grow spiritually. A stunted Christian who fails to grow remains vulnerable to fears, doubts and unbelief.

Salvation is not just a momentary event when a person passes from death to life and from darkness to light. Salvation is in reality a three-fold event that takes place in three distinct tenses: past, present and future.

Birth is a momentary experience. One moment a baby does not have life in this world; the next moment he lives and breathes as a new born infant. When the new birth takes place in a moment of time, a person is justified by grace through faith. This we call the past tense of salvation when the person is **saved from the penalty of sin**. As Scripture teaches, *"Therefore, there is no condemnation for those who are in Christ Jesus"* (Ro 8:1). The Christian need not fear eternal damnation for he or she is secure in Christ. That part of salvation is finished! It is past.

Conversion, however, is only the first part of salvation. Peter speaks of "growing" up in our salvation (1 Pe 2:2). During the ensuing life of the Christian, a believer is **being saved from the power of sin.** This is an on-going, continuing process in life which is called "sanctification."

The Christian must contend with the world, the flesh and the devil: the **world** is hostile to everything Christ-centred; the **flesh is** the "old sinful nature" which is enticed by temptations from the world; and the **devil** is like a roaring lion who seeks out weak Christians to tempt them to sin.

Therefore, in this world the Christian needs to be strong in order to resist the world, the flesh and the devil; he or she needs to *"grow up to salvation."*

The future tense of our salvation will take place at the return of Christ when all Christians will be raised from the dead, given new, resurrected bodies with sinless natures and will be forever **separated from the very presence of sin.**

The purpose of this chapter is to explore the ways in which a baby in Christ grows spiritually into full maturity.

The three essentials for every infant to grow into maturity are breathing, feeding, and exercising. In the same way, every Christian needs to breathe, feed, and exercise in order to mature as a believer.

FEEDNG ON THE WORD OF GOD

The Word of God is just as essential to the health and well-being of a Christian as food is necessary for a human being. A normal, healthy person is hungry and desires to eat. A live, healthy Christian loves God's Word and is eager to meditate on Scripture.

David treasured the words of God, saying, *"More to be desired are they than gold, even much fine gold; sweeter also than honey and the drippings of the honeycomb"* (Ps 19:10). The Psalmist said, *"How sweet are your words to my taste, sweeter than honey to my mouth"* (Ps 119:103).

Job loved the Lord and faithfully followed his commandments. For him God's Word was more valuable than his daily food for he said: *"I have treasured the words of his mouth more than my portion of food"* (Job 23:12).

After the prophet Jeremiah "ate" the words of God he said, *"Your words became to me a joy and the delight of my heart"* (Jer 15:16).

David vividly describes the person whom God blesses in this life:

"Blessed is the man who does not walk in the counsel of the wicked
or stand in the way of sinners or sit in the seat of mockers.
But his delight is in the law of the LORD,
and his law he meditates day and night.
He is like a tree planted by streams of water,

which yields its fruit in season and whose leaf does not wither.
Whatever he does prospers" (Ps 1:1-3).

Importance of the Word of God

The Bible teaches that reading, studying, meditating, memorizing and obeying the Word of God is essential for any Christian to grow strong in faith and thereby resist temptation and overcome the fear of death.

Like newborn babies,
you must crave pure spiritual milk
so that you will grow into a full experience of salvation.
Cry out for this nourishment
(1 Pe 2:2 *NLT*).

Derived from this verse we learn the following:

We ought to crave the Word of God: New born babies are hungry all the time. Their tiny bodies need continual nourishment of the mother's milk in order to grow. One might say that their early months are devoted entirely to sleeping and drinking the mother's milk.

In the same way all Christians are commanded to long for the "pure spiritual milk" of the Word of God. As babies naturally crave for milk, so Christians should do likewise. But if for any reason there isn't a natural desire, Peter *commands* that believers should cry out for God's Word.

And the purpose is so that they might grow up as Christians. They ought not remain as immature, undeveloped believers. In the previous verse (1 Pe 2:1) Peter admonishes believers to put away malice, deceit, hypocrisy, envy and all slander. These practices are natural for unbelievers but ought not to be found among believers. In order to grow strong as Christians to live a godly life, they must (a command) drink deeply from the Word of God for nourishment so that they can resist the hateful talk and works of the flesh.

We need to grow up in our salvation: Growth follows conversion. Sad to say, spiritual growth is not an accomplished fact in every Christian. Many remain infantile even in old age. They are weak and fall into many temptations. They display much of the old self.

The Corinthian Church is such an example. Paul did not consider them "spiritual people" but "people of the flesh," that is, carnal (fleshly – *"you are still controlled by your sinful nature" NLT*). Though older in the faith, they still needed "milk," the food for babies, not the "solid food" that adults eat (1 Co 3:1-2).

Paul was writing to a people in the Greek culture and used "milk" and "solid food" in a figurative manner. Various cultures thrive on milk and other liquids as adults. But the picture is clear. The Corinthian Church was weak and fleshly because they had not grown up as spiritually mature Christians. The reason? They did not crave the Word of God.

Many churches today, like the church in Corinth, are filled with jealousy and strife, dividing themselves into different competing groups instead of humbly serving the Lord. Churches with leadership fights, ambitions, power struggles and greed betray their spiritual weakness. They fail to nourish themselves on the Word of God. They are still controlled by their sinful nature.

God's Command to Grow

Because of dangers lurking and threatening the Christian, God commands believers to grow in grace and in the knowledge of our Lord and Saviour.

"But you, my friends whom I love, are forewarned,
and should therefore be very careful not to be carried away by the errors of
wicked men and so lose your proper foothold.
On the contrary,
you should grow in grace
and in your knowledge of our Lord and Saviour Jesus Christ –
to him be glory now and until the dawning of the day of eternity"
(2 Pe 3:17-18 Phillips).

Derived from this verse we learn the following:

False teaching abounds: These verses are the last inspired words of the apostle Peter before he was martyred as a Christian (crucified upside down in Rome). Therefore, they bear special importance for us.

Looking into the future after his departure from this life, Peter foresaw the danger of heresies and false teaching by men who distort the Scriptures. Error usually contains partial truth. It is not easy to detect. Many Christians are fooled. False teachers quote from Scripture, but take verses out of context. They twist, misrepresent and alter the meaning of Scripture. They fail to teach the whole Word of God and emphasize only a partial truth and thereby misrepresent what God says.

Therefore, Peter commands the readers to be on guard ["be very careful"] "not to be carried away by the error of lawless men." To be forewarned is to be forearmed. Knowing that false teachers will distort the Word of God can help prepare the believer.

The Protestant Reformers of the 16th century, including Martin Luther and John Calvin, were deeply troubled by the established Church which had gone astray because they included church tradition equal with the Scriptures. Whenever the Church defended such teachings as purgatory, indulgences, prayers to and for the dead, Mariolatry, and works-righteousness, they cited church tradition.

The rallying cry of all the Reformers was "Scripture Alone." This remains a distinctive of evangelicals today. Scripture is our final authority. By Scripture alone we can discern between truth and error.

False teachers promote their propaganda and cite Scripture, but they deceitfully distort and misrepresent what Scripture teaches. They pick and choose verses and ignore the immediate context and the larger context of the whole of Scriptures.

Only mature believers who know the Scriptures well and who are strengthened and enlightened by the Holy Spirit can discern the truth.

Growing is Important: Peter closes his final letter with these two commands: (1) "be on your guard" ("be very careful") so as not to carried away blindly along with others; (2) and "grow..."

Instead of being carried away into error, Peter commands his readers to "grow in grace and in the knowledge" of Christ.

Spiritual Insight is Needed when Meditating on Scripture

As important as the Bible is in the growth of a Christian, a believer must go beyond the mere academic study of the Bible, and gain a spiritual understanding into its relevance and application to life.

> *For this reason, since the day we heard about you,*
> *have not stopped praying for you*
> *and <u>asking God to fill you with the knowledge of his will</u>*
> *<u>through spiritual wisdom and understanding</u>.*
> *And we pray this in order that you may live a life worthy of the Lord*
> *And may please him in every way:*
> *bearing fruit in every good work, growing in the knowledge of God,*
> *being strengthened with all power according to his glorious might*
> *so that you may have great endurance and patience...* (Col 1:9-11).

From these verses we learn the following:

The need to know God's will with spiritual understanding: After the apostle Paul heard that people in the city of Colosse had been converted to Christ, he began praying for them that they might be filled with the knowledge of God's will *through spiritual wisdom and understanding*. This knowledge can be found only in the Holy Scriptures and by the help of the Holy Spirit.

Principles of biblical interpretation should be based on the understanding of vocabulary and grammar in the literary context and historical setting, interpreting the meaning of words according to their natural import. We must *exegete* ("read out" of the text) the meaning that the authors intended and never *eisegete* ("read into" the text) any meaning the authors never intended. In one sense, we interpret the Holy Writings very similar to other writings, but with the belief that the Holy Spirit has inspired all the biblical writers resulting in unity of Scripture. There are no conflicting theologies in the Bible. We interpret the Bible by comparing Scripture with Scripture.

But a true knowledge of God's will requires spiritual wisdom and discernment to know God and his will. This is possible only through the illumination of the Spirit who indwells every believer.

In 1 Corinthians 2:10-15 Paul explained the importance of the Spirit illuminating our minds so that we may understand the spiritual meaning of the Scriptures.

> *For who could really understand a man's inmost thoughts*
> *except the spirit of man himself?*
> *How much less could anyone understand the thoughts of God*
> *except the very Spirit of God?*
> *And the marvelous thing is this,*
> *that we now receive not the spirit of the world but the Spirit of God himself,*
> *so that we can actually understand*
> *something of God's generosity toward us.*

Unbelievers without the Holy Spirit cannot understand the spiritual meaning of Scriptures and its application to their lives. But once a person is converted and born of the Spirit of God, the Holy Spirit comes to dwell within the believer and He begins shedding light on the meaning and application of Scriptures. As we read further in 1 Corinthians 2:14-15 Phillips translation:

> *But the unspiritual man simply cannot accept the matters which the Spirit deals with – they just don't make sense to him,*
> *for, after all, you must be spiritual to see spiritual things.*
> *The spiritual man, on the other hand, has an insight into the meaning of everything, though his insight may baffle the man of the world.*
> (I Co 2:6-14 *Phillips*)

In humility the believer prays for spiritual understanding as he searches the Scriptures. The most important truths that God desires us to know are plainly and clearly revealed in the Bible. Many teachings, however, are more difficult to understand. Even the apostle Peter found the writings of Paul "hard to understand" (2 Pe 3:16). A fuller understanding takes time, study and reflection. The Bible has such deep riches that we learn more and more from the same biblical passages as the years pass by. We never fully understand all that is found in the Bible and believers often disagree in their understanding of Scriptures.

The purpose of knowing the Scriptures: A knowledge of the will of God found in the Scriptures was not the full desire of Paul. The purpose was that believers might please the Lord Jesus Christ who had saved them, and might obey him, and bear fruit in every good work, and "*might grow in the knowledge of God.*"

Knowing God and pleasing God and growing in faith as Christians are not possible apart from reading, studying, meditating on and memorizing God's Word. As the Psalmist says, "*How can a young man keep his way pure? By living according to your word.*" "*I have hidden your word in my heart that I might not sin against you*" (Ps 119:9, 11).

BREATHING IN PRAYER

Breathing must be constant and uninterrupted or else we die. We don't breathe just in the morning or in the evening or before we eat. If a person does not breathe all the time, his heart stops beating, he becomes brain dead and his corpse is laid to rest.

Prayer is a Constant Practice

Prayer, like breathing, should be continuous. The Bible teaches, be "constant in prayer" (Ro 12:12 *ESV*). Elsewhere we read, "Pray without ceasing" (1 Th 5:16).

So what is prayer? How can we possibly "pray without ceasing"? Prayer is talking to God; it is communing with our Lord and Saviour; it is fellowshipping with him. Prayer is opening our hearts to God; it is the breath of the soul. Without prayer, the spiritual life will perish.

"To pray" means literally, "to ask" or "to beg." That is what we associate with prayer. "Ask and it will be given you" (Mt 7:7). Whenever we pray, we beg God for help in one way or another because we feel helpless and are in great need. Many people never pray unless they desperately need or want something. God does not pray because he is all-sufficient. We pray because we are weak and needy.

But prayer is much more than asking God for help. Prayer includes worship with thanksgiving, praise and adoration. Prayer involves confession of sins. Prayer is petition for others in need. Jesus taught us how to pray with all these elements in the Lord's Prayer (Mt 6:9-13).

But if prayer should be "constant" and "without ceasing," it must be much more. Prayer is an ever present reliance on God, trusting him, thanking him, seeking his help, confessing sins. Christians should live with an ever conscious presence of God. Whether we are working, resting, walking, playing or studying, we are conscious of the presence of God and relying on him. As we pass through each day we are conscious of God's will and seek God's help when tempted, confess our sins when we fall short of his will, ask him for guidance and wisdom, rejoice and give thanks for his blessings.

Prayer cannot be separated from feeding on God's Word. Neither can God's Word be separated from prayer. They go hand in hand. We pray as we read the Scriptures, and we are guided by the Scriptures as we pray. Through prayer we commune with God and through the Scriptures we hear God speak to us.

As important as it is to pray without ceasing, experience has shown that we need to devote a time period during each day to read and meditate on God's Word and to pray. This is a spiritual discipline necessary for spiritual growth. "Praying without ceasing" can become an excuse to neglect a focused, concentrated time with the Lord in what may be called, "personal devotions."

Jesus admonished his disciples, *"But when you pray, go into your room, close the door and pray to your Father who is unseen"* (Mt 6:6). Choosing a time when you can withdraw from the business of life to spend time with God is most important.

When should we read God's Word? When do we offer God our uninterrupted worship and praise and when do we intercede for others? The people of Israel, both in the Old Testament and New Testament, prayed three times daily: 9:00 A.M., 12:00 noon, and 3:00 P.M. Daniel "got down on his knees and prayed, giving thanks to his God..." three times a day (Da 6:10). Peter and John went to the temple at the time of prayer at 3:00 in the afternoon (Ac 3:1). However, no command is found anywhere in Scripture as to the time or duration of our personal devotions.

Spending time with God daily in prayerful meditation on his Word is a spiritual discipline which reaps rich dividends. But it should not be considered a legalistic requirement to please God. Rather, it is a means of grace when God pours out his favour on our lives to live each day for him. Following are suggestions for developing a faithful, regular time of "personal devotions."

If at all possible, the early morning hour, before work and the business of the day, has proven to be the best time. Devotions held as the first thing in the morning ensures that the interruptions of the day will not interfere with your time with the Lord. It also prepares one for the challenges of the day. If for any reason the early hours are not the best, you need to choose a time that becomes a regular, habitual time when you "enter into your room," wherever and whatever that might be, so you can be alone with your God.

God intends his children to know and feel that Christ is near them, that Christ continues to love and care for them, even in times of sickness. This is only possible when Christians breathe constantly in prayer.

If Christians are not walking close to the Lord, they may feel that God is not near them. When sickness and death strike, they quickly "pray" for help, but when God does not answer immediately, they may turn to the "witchdoctor" and other traditional resources.

The Christian faith is often in name only. They are "Christians" because their parents are Christian, or because their custom is to attend church services on Sunday. Only someone who is born again by the Spirit of God, and who lives a life of prayer, can know and trust the presence of God in times of trouble.

"Without faith it is impossible to please God" (Heb 11:6). In African Traditional Religion the peoples used magic and help from witchdoctors for their own benefit. Magic served them. But Christians cannot use God for their benefit. Prayer is not some form of magic that quickly makes God do what you want. Prayer is communion and fellowship with the eternal, all wise and all loving God, the Creator whose glory is paramount. That means that your faith in times of trouble will glorify him because you trust him. Quickly answered prayer does not glorify God as much as patient, humble trust.

Habakkuk was troubled. He was unhappy with God, so he prayed: "How long, O LORD, must I call for help, but you do not listen"? (Hab 1:2). Christians often ask, "Why?" We cannot understand the reasons for the sickness or other troubles. Often God seems unfair and unjust! Though God does not always answer our prayers as we want, a mature Christian learns to trust in God's love and wisdom. In the end, Habbakuk surrendered to God in trust as he prayed:

Though the fig tree does not bud
and there are not grapes on the vines,
though the olive crop fails and the fields produce no food,
though there are no sheep in the pen and no cattle in the stalls,
yet I will rejoice in the LORD, I will be joyful in God my Saviour.
The Sovereign LORD is my strength;
he makes my feet like the feet of a deer,
he enables me to go on the heights (Hab 3:17-19).

That kind of faith is awesome and glorifies God. But such faith is only possible when the person has grown strong and matures in his knowledge of God through prayer and the reading of God's Word.

Paul was troubled by "a thorn in the flesh" which was probably some kind of physical illness (2 Co 12:1-10). Though Paul prayed three times that this thorn would be removed, God denied his request. God is not always pleased to heal, and this is not necessarily due to our lack of faith or the presence of sin in our lives. Instead, God taught Paul patience, endurance, and greater trust. God's reply was this: *"My grace is sufficient for you, for my power is made perfect in weakness."*

Job was severely tested, even though he was righteous in God's sight. All his possessions were destroyed and all his children died, but Job never cursed God. In faith he declared, *"He knows the way that I take; when he has tested me, I will come forth as gold"* (Job 23:10).

A Christian who grows in his knowledge of the Lord through a disciplined life of prayer and meditation on the Word of God becomes a mature Christian. He learns to submit to the will of God because he trusts God.

Before dying on the cross, Jesus submitted to his Father's will and prayed, *"My Father, if it is possible, may this cup be taken from me. Yet not as I will, but as you will."* Because Jesus humbled himself to the point of death on the cross, *"God exalted him to the highest place and gave him the name that is above every name"* (Php 2:9). In the same way, God will reward his children who trust and obey.

God may test his children through trials and difficulties, but his purposes and plans for us are good. God's promise is very comforting. *"'For I know the plans I have for you,' declares the LORD, 'plans to prosper you and not to harm you, plans to give you hope and a future'"* (Jer 29:11). When we persevere in faith believing, through God's enabling grace, he promises us unspeakably great blessings in the ages to come.

Prayer Is Like Exhaling and Inhaling

Human beings breathe out in order to exhale from the lungs stale air with carbon dioxide and nitrogen, and inhale oxygen to sustain the life-giving process of metabolism. Oxygen is a colorless gas that is life sustaining, but carbon dioxide is a colorless gas that in large amounts leads to dizziness, confusion, headaches and eventual death.

Breathing is therefore essential for physical life in order to rid the body of toxicants, and to absorb life giving oxygen that builds.

Exhaling: "Breathing out" may therefore be compared to the spiritual breathing of repenting (exhaling). Sin is a toxicant that displeases God; it destroys fellowship with God and causes great harm to the person. The harm includes a guilty conscience, lost joy, and broken relationships with God and others. It also weakens the person's ability to resist temptation.

Unconfessed sin grieves the Holy Spirit; it will "offend, vex or sadden Him" (Eph 4:30 *Amplified*). In the context Paul says, *"Watch the way you talk. Let nothing foul or dirty come out of your mouth. Say only what helps, each word a gift"* (Eph 4:29 *The MESSAGE*). He warns against slander, bitterness, malice, rage and anger. Repentance is needed whenever we speak in a manner that does not please God.

Repentance is essential for the spiritual health of a Christian.

God's promise is trustworthy: *"If we confess our sins, he is faithful and just and will forgive our sins and purify us from all unrighteousness"* (1 Jn 1:9). After being sorry for sin, confessing, and repenting, the believer ought not to feel guilty any more. *"The blood of Jesus cleanses from all sin."*

Inhaling: "Breathing in" may be compared to the daily prayer for the Holy Spirit to fill, empower and guide. Every believer is indwelled by the Holy Spirit who will never abandon the believer. But the filling of the Holy Spirit should be a daily experience.

> *Do not get drunk on wine, which leads to debauchery.*
> *Instead, be filled with the Spirit.*
> *Speak to one another with psalms, hymns and spiritual songs.*
> *Sing and make music in your heart to the Lord...* (Eph 5:18-19).

The verb, "be filled," is a command in the present tense that indicates a continuing, ongoing imperative of "being filled." So the meaning is, "You must continue on being filled with the Holy Spirit."

This is very different from the gift of the Spirit upon conversion which is instantaneous and final upon faith in Christ. Paul makes it very clear that every believer without exception has been given the Holy Spirit at the time of his conversion (Ro 8:9).

The Spirit is God's seal upon every believer, *"a deposit guaranteeing our inheritance"* (Eph 1:13-14). The presence of the Spirit in the believer can never depart.

But the command in Ephesians 5, *"continue being filled,"* is a daily exercise and command. In that text a comparison is made between being drunk with wine and being continually filled with the Holy Spirit. Just as a person under the influence of wine is controlled by the wine, so a person filled with the Spirit is influenced and controlled by the Spirit. Throughout Scripture we see instances of the Spirit empowering, gifting and enabling God's people to do exploits for him.

When filled by the Spirit the believer is marked by the fruit of the Spirit: *"love, joy, peace, patience, kindness, goodness, faithfulness, gentleness and self-control"* (Gal 5:22-23).

But when we are not filled by the Spirit daily, we may fall into old habits and follow the ways of our fleshly, sinful nature. Christians are commanded to live by the the Spirit.

So I say, <u>live by the Spirit,</u>
<u>and you will not gratify the desires of the sinful nature</u>.
For the sinful nature desires what is contrary to the Spirit,
and the Spirit what is is contrary to the sinful nature.
They are in conflict with each other, so that you do not do what you want.
But if you are led by the Spirit, you are not under law.
<u>The acts of the sinful nature are obvious</u>:
sexual immorality, impurity and debauchery; idolatry and witchcraft;
hatred, discord, jealousy, fits of rage, selfish ambition,
dissensions, factions and envy;
drunkenness, orgies, and the like.
I warn you, as I did before,
that those who live like this will not inherit the kingdom of God"
(Gal 5:16-21).

Notice the clusters of sinful behavior, each separated by a colon (;). Each successive cluster begins with the words: sexual immorality, idolatry, hatred and drunkenness. Those clusters are problems with Christians today.

But the largest cluster with the most words, which is perhaps the most visible problem in churches today, begins with "hatred" and includes: *hatred, discord, jealousy, fits of rage, selfish ambition, dissensions, factions and envy.* If the Christian Church would live by the Holy Spirit and not live carnal, fleshly lives, the testimony before the world would be dramatic. All discord, envy, and selfish ambition that leads to leadership struggles would be replaced by love.

How then are Christians to be filled daily by the Spirit? Through faith we received Christ as our Saviour and through faith we are filled by the Spirit daily. Paul reminds us, *"<u>Just as you received Christ Jesus as Lord, continue to live in him,</u> rooted and built up in him, strengthened in the faith as you were taught, and overflowing with thankfulness"* (Col 2:6-7).

You received Christ by faith. You now continue to live daily by faith, asking the Holy Spirit by faith to fill you daily so that he will control you. Many

Christians feel that they must weep, fast, beg and plead for the Holy Spirit to fill them. They are so misguided. They do not understand that *"we live by faith"* (Ro 1:17). We are not saved by human effort of fasting, begging, pleading and weeping. Nor do Christians grow in their walk with the Lord in that way. Salvation is not gained through human effort. Salvation is by faith alone, and living by the Spirit is no different.

EXERCISING SPIRITUALLY

When babies cry, they stretch their muscles and this helps them grow. When teenagers play football, they strengthen their muscles. Sedentary adults, who sit all day in the office, then ride the bus back home and lounge in their house at night, are shortening their life span because they are not exercising. The heart is a muscle that atrophies – withers and shrivels – unless it is used. Sitting all day is bad for physical health. Life spans are shortened with inactivity.

In the same way, a believer in Christ who does not exercise spiritually will remain weak and unproductive. A believer who simply goes to church on Sundays cannot grow healthy and strong in his faith.

Following are the necessary exercises of a Christian to bring growth and maturity:

Exercising Faith

Without exercise the physical muscles are not stretched and strengthened, and without trials and tests in life faith cannot grow. Faith is exercised and greatly strengthened whenever the believer endures afflictions of various kind.

> *When all kinds of trials and temptations crowd into your lives, my brothers,*
> *don't resent them as intruders, but welcome them as friends!*
> *Realize that they come to test your faith*
> *and to produce in you the quality of endurance.*
> *But let the process go on*
> *until that endurance is fully developed,*
> *and you will find you have become men of mature character*
> *with the right sort of independence (Jas 1:2ff Phillips).*

What this Scripture teaches is the opposite of what is taught by preachers of the Prosperity Gospel, sometimes known as the "Health and Wealth Gospel." This false gospel is attracting masses of Christians in Africa. They teach that God's will for his children is always that they be healthy and wealthy. The impression is given that if a Christian has enough faith he will prosper materially and experience no trials. If someone is struggling financially or is troubled with various trials, it is because he lacks faith.

Furthermore, they teach that faith, donations, and positive speech will automatically bring wealth. Followers of these preachers are urged to give generously as seed money so that their own wealth will increase. The scandal is that the preacher becomes wealthy while the members become poor.

This serious error is leading many Christians astray. These preachers have never studied their Bible carefully. They distort and twist what God has said. They take verses out of context in isolation of what the whole of Scriptures teach.

For these preachers God is a puppet who is manipulated to do whatever the Christian desires. This is the magic of Traditional African Religion. Magic says, "My will be done," but the Christian who worships the almighty, all-wise and all-loving Creator and Saviour, prays, *"Not my will but your will be done."*

Instead of promising health and wealth for the Christian, God's Word promises trials and testings in order to strengthen faith. The crying of the baby and movement of his arms and legs are baby exercises. But that baby needs to grow and the only way he will grow is with more exercising.

According to the Bible (Jas 1:2ff), the only way you will become mature in character as Christians is if your faith is tested with trials. *"All kinds of trials and temptations"* may include lack of income, financial distress, sickness, family problems, work related issues, famine, an unsaved spouse, wayward children and the like.

When these trials come our faith is challenged. Does God really love me? Is my Christian faith really worth keeping? Should I try some traditional remedies for my problems like going to the "witchdoctor"? As one trusts God more and more, our faith grows stronger and stronger. The end result is growth into maturity as believers.

Thank God, the God and Father of our Lord Jesus Christ,
that in his great mercy we have been <u>*born again into a life full of hope,*</u>
through Christ's rising again from the dead!...
This means tremendous joy to you, I know,
even though at present you are temporarily harassed
by all kinds of trials and temptations.
<u>*This is no accident – it happens to prove your faith,*</u>
<u>*which is infinitely more valuable than gold,*</u>
and gold, as you know, even though it is ultimately perishable,
must be purified by fire.
<u>*This proving of your faith is planned*</u>

to result in praise and honour and glory
in the day when Jesus Christ reveals himself...
The man who patiently endures the temptations and trials
that come to him is the truly happy man.
For once his testing is complete
he will receive the crown of life
which the Lord has promised to all who love him.
(1 Pe 1:3, 6-7 *Phillips*).

Trials not only strengthen faith; they prove whether faith is genuine and result in "the crown of life." Not all those who profess to be Christians are really Christians because not all faith is genuine faith. Tests and trials in the life of a Christian are no accident. God has planned them in order to prove and demonstrate that our faith is genuine. This saving faith is more precious than refined gold that perishes because saving faith results in eternal glory to God for his amazing grace that saves undeserving sinners like we are.

Exercising by Abiding in Christ

Closely associated with the exercise of faith is the command to "abide in Christ" (Jn 15:1-10).

Just before his crucifixion, Jesus gathered the Twelve in an upper room (Lk 22:12) and shared deep thoughts to prepare his apostles for his departure. The allegory of the Vine and Branches was told in the Upper Room Discourse found in John 13-17. To understand the significance of Jesus' teaching on the Vine and the Branches, we need to consider the context.

The time spent in the upper room was Jesus' last opportunity to teach his disciples before his death. These men had been with Jesus for three years. But during those last precious hours with Jesus, Judas Iscariot left the disciples in order to arrange with the Jewish leaders for his betrayal of Jesus (Jn 13:18-30). After Judas' departure Jesus took the opportunity to exhort his apostles not to desert him but to remain with him.

With that in mind, we read the allegory of the Vine and the Branches:

I am the true vine, and my Father is the vinedresser.
Every branch in Me that does not bear fruit, He takes away;
and every branch that bears fruit,
He prunes it so that it may bear more fruit
You are already clean because of the word I have spoken to you.
Abide in Me and I in you.
As a branch cannot bear fruit of itself unless it abides in the vine,
so neither can you unless you abide in Me.

I am the vine, you are the branches;
He who abides in Me and I in him, he bears much fruit,
for apart from Me you can do nothing.
If anyone does not abide in Me,
he is thrown away as a branch and dries up;
and they gather them, and cast them into the fire and they are burned.
If you abide in Me, and my words abide in you, ask whatever you wish,
and it will be done for you.
My Father is glorified by this, that you bear much fruit,
and so prove to be My disciples.
Just as the Father has loved Me, I have also loved you;
abide in My love.
If you keep my commandments, you will abide in My love;
Just as I have kept My Father's commandments and abide in His love.
(Jn 15:1-10 *NASB*)

In this allegory we need to focus on the central teaching. The key word is, "ABIDE." Literally, the Greek word means to "stay, live, dwell, or lodge" in a particular place. Figuratively, it refers to someone who does not leave the realm or sphere in which he finds himself – he "remains, continues, abides."

Bible translations and paraphrases use various words to express this thought of abiding: "remain," "dwell," "live in me," "joined to the vine," "make yourself at home with me," "continue in me," "growing in me," "shares my life," "live your life in me" and "abide."

Jesus is the vine and apart from *remaining in him*, his disciples can do nothing of eternal value. One cannot help believe that Judas' departure formed the background for this allegory. On other occasions many of Jesus' followers deserted him because of his teaching. Now, one of the Twelve deserted Jesus and worse; he was about to betray him. Jesus warned the Twelve to remain.

However, the allegory goes much deeper. The disciples were told, *"remain and dwell in me."* As the branch is vitally attached to the vine in order to receive nourishment from the vine, so the disciples must *make their home in Jesus*, drawing spiritual strength from him in order to bear fruit.

Earlier Jesus had taught this intimate union with Christ. *"I am in the Father, and you are in me, and I am in you"* (Jn 14:20). Frequently, the New Testament affirms that the believer is *in Christ* and Christ is *in the believer*. God is Spirit and the Triune God indwells the believer – Father, Son and Holy Spirit. This is a mystical union which is difficult for human beings to grasp.

In practice, how do we *abide in Christ?* In verse seven Jesus speaks of the believer abiding in Christ and his words abiding in the believer. In verse nine Jesus says, *"Abide in my love. If you keep my commandments, you will abide in my love."* Abiding in Christ cannot be separated from both knowing and obeying Jesus' commandments. Loving Christ with all of our hearts means that our lives centre on Jesus as we worship him and rely on him to live a life pleasing to him. Obedience is not possible unless we have that intimate communion with Jesus, depending on him to help us obey and please him.

Hence, abiding in Christ is closely connected with trusting him, being constant in prayer and meditating on God's Word. Abiding in Christ is a personal, intimate relationship with Christ, depending on him by faith for all of life.

One should not assume that verse two teaches the possibility of losing salvation when Jesus says, *"Every branch in Me that does not bear fruit, He takes away."* We have seen elsewhere that the Bible clearly teaches that a person who is born again by the Spirit of God <u>cannot </u>lose his relationship with God. Perhaps he is alluding to Judas who <u>appeared</u> to be remaining in Jesus, but was not. In the end Judas failed to produce the fruit of abiding faith and perseverance.

What this allegory does teach is that believers are responsible to exercise their faith and obedience for their growth in grace. Maturity will not take place and God cannot be pleased if a Christian fails to exercise his privileges and responsibilities of trusting Christ in all situations, praying without ceasing, meditating on and obeying God's Word and <u>remaining in Christ</u> who is the only source of the strength we need to live a life worthy of our calling.

Exercising by Guarding the Heart

Solomon, the wisest man who ever lived, gave sound advice which he himself failed to follow: "<u>Above all else, guard your heart</u>, for it is the wellspring of life" (Pr 43:23).

The context refers to the teachings that Solomon gave his son. They are not simply memorized so that they can be repeated back like a parrot. They were to be pondered and assimilated into the centre of one's being, namely, the "heart." In Hebrew the "heart" includes the totality of the inner person – the emotions, the intellect and the moral faculties.

Jesus teaches the same truth:

> No good tree bears bad fruit, nor does a bad tree bear good fruit.
> Each tree is recognized by its own fruit.
> People do not pick figs from thornbushes, or grapes from briers.

The good man brings good things out of the good stored up in his heart, and the evil man brings evil things out of the evil stored up in his heart. For out of the overflow of his heart his mouth speaks (Lk 6:43-45).

How do we store up things in our hearts? Through the eye gate and the ear gate we admit thoughts and ideas into our inner chambers which stimulate our own motives, aspirations and emotions. It's not as if the heart is innocent and pure from birth and only becomes corrupt through external contaminations. The Bible teaches that the heart is sinful from birth. But the inner self continues to store up more and more through the eyes and ears.

Solomon advised that the "heart" must be guarded above everything else for "it is the wellspring of life." In the words of Jesus, "*What you say comes from what is in your heart*" (Lk 6:45 NLT).

We wear shoes to protect our feet from injury, and clothes to protect the body from cold. Ancient warriors protected their heads with helmets, and body armour to protect their vital organs. But what protects the "heart"?

We guard our hearts in part by guarding our eyes and ears. We protect them from what is displeasing to God. Since we are called to live in this world, we cannot live in a bubble of holiness. We are surrounded on every side by evil. But there is much that we can do to *guard* our eyes and ears. We can make the deliberate choice that we will not willingly listen to anything or choose to watch anything that does not glorify God or edify us in the Lord.

The internet is a marvelous technological masterpiece of ingenuity. Through search engines we can find anything we want on-line. Unfortunately, Africa has been made vulnerable along with the rest of the world with the on-line pornography available. This immoral trash is ruining the minds of millions of men and women, young girls and boys, including pastors.

Pornography appeals to our fallen natures. Like alcohol and drugs, it is addictive. And the law of diminishing returns applies to pornography as well. The more you see, the more you want and the more you need. It is exciting, titillating and pleasing to our sinful natures. You think of it all day long and into the night. It ruins marriages and destroys lives.

But pornography is not the only thing that contaminates the heart through the eye and ear gates. All kinds of sensuous, violent and ungodly portrayals are made in movies, theater, TV, pop music, magazines, cell phones and smart phones. They can fill the heart with all kinds of evil thoughts and should be guarded against.

The apostle Paul lays out the standard to determine what we should allow our thoughts to dwell on, what we should allow to enter our ear and eye gates.

And now, dear brothers and sisters, one final thing.
Fix your thoughts on what is true, and honourable, and right, and pure,
and lovely, and admirable.
Think about things that are excellent and worthy of praise (Php 4:8 *NLT*).

Entertaining moral filth in the life of any Christian, weakens them spiritually. When we fail to guard our hearts and allow sinful thoughts to take root, this becomes an invitation to Satan to tempt us even more. A person without adequate sleep and proper nourishment from food becomes weakened physically and opens the door to all kinds of illnesses. In the same way, anyone who does not guard his heart will find himself more vulnerable to fear and unbelief. If a Christian desires to please God by trusting him during times of sickness and misfortune, he must diligently guard his heart.

Exercising by Serving Others with Spiritual Gifts

Life in Africa has always been in relationships. In fact, one of the strongest forces in African culture is a deep sense of kinship. "I am because we are" is the common way of looking at individual Africans. Over several centuries westerners have become very individualistic due to industrialization, urbanization and mobility. But such individualism is foreign to the African traditional life style. As industry moves into Africa and cities grow in size, we see the gradual breakdown of the extended family. The traditional emphasis on relationships should be cherished and maintained because it is the biblical way of life.

But more important than the natural kinship is the spiritual family of God. A Christian is part of a body, the Body of Christ (1 Co 12:1-31). He is a member of the household of God. Every believer should become part of the fellowship of a church, not just as a church attender, but as an actively functioning member of the family of God. Brothers and sisters in Christ are closer to one another (or should be closer) than to family members who know not the Lord.

Believers have been saved in order to serve. Many Christians, if not most, are simply church attenders. Rather than coming late to church and sitting in the back, a healthy, growing Christian should be vitally involved in the church by using spiritual gifts for the edification of believers.

Most Christians, however, are unaware of the spiritual gifts that God has given them. They have not exercised their faith in the use of their spiritual gifts for the edification of the believers.

They are like the Dead Sea in the Holy Land which only receives fresh water from the Jordan River but has no outlet. Hence, the Dead Sea is literally *dead* with no live fish. Instead, God desires all believers to be like the Sea of Galilee which has fresh water flowing in and flowing out into the Jordan River. Hence, the Sea of Galilee is alive with thousands of fish. When Christians give out by edifying others with their spiritual gifts, they become healthier.

In order to be a thriving, growing Christian, every believer needs to be active in both attending and serving in his local church with his or her gifts.

> *Don't think you are better than you really are.*
> *Be honest in your evaluation of yourselves,*
> *measuring yourselves by the faith God has given us.*
> *Just as our bodies have many parts and each part has a special function,*
> *so it is with Christ's body.*
> *We are many parts of one body, and we all belong to each other.*
> *In his grace, God has given us different gifts for doing certain things well.*
> *So if God has given you the ability to prophesy,*
> *speak out with as much faith as God has given you.*
> *If your gift is serving others, serve them well.*
> *If you are a teacher, teach well.*
> *If your gift is to encourage others, be encouraging.*
> *If it is giving, give generously.*
> *If God has given you leadership ability, take the responsibility seriously.*
> *And if you have a gift for showing kindness to others, do it gladly.*
> (Ro 12:3-8 *NLT*).

The apostle Paul compares the Church of Jesus Christ to the human body which has many members (eyes, ears, mouth, feet etc.). Each member is needed. If everyone were the head, how could the body move? If everyone were a hand, how could the body see? Each member has a different function with differing gifts given by God's grace. The spiritual gifts which Paul mentions in Romans 12, I Corinthians 12-14 and Ephesians 4:11 are not all inclusive but representative of many gifts God has granted to all believers.

The problem, which the Christian Church had in Paul's day, persists to this day. Christians valued certain gifts above others. They were jealous of one another and strove to exercise the "best" and "greatest" gift.

So Paul begins by exhorting everyone to be humble – *"Don't think you are better than you really are."* Elsewhere Paul admonishes, *"Do nothing from rivalry or conceit, but in humility count others more significant than yourselves"* (Php 2:3 *ESV*). That is a powerful exhortation: *"count others more significant than yourselves."* By grace we have been made members of the Body of Christ, and it is by grace that we have been gifted by God. Our responsibility is to use our gifts with gratitude to God and a desire to bless others – and not strive to be "the big man."

All faith is by God's grace whether it is saving faith or serving faith. God has granted us both the faith and the measure of faith to embrace the spiritual gifts with which we are endowed. Blessed are those who are active in their faith and use their gifts for the glory of God and the edification of the Church.

This is an amazing truth. Those Christians who minister to others, who exercise their faith and their gifts for the benefit of others, grow spiritually and become more blessed than those to whom they minister. And in the process of growing spiritually and growing in the knowledge of God, they lose the fear of death because they know and trust in the One who saved them.

Exercising by Witnessing

Faith is exercised when we witness to others and tell them what Jesus has done for us. Witnessing is not preaching from the Bible or giving a doctrinal explanation of salvation; it is a personal testimony of what we have seen and known by experience in coming to faith in Christ.

The early disciples of Christ are perfect examples. Andrew, Simon Peter's brother, spent a day with Jesus after John the Baptist pointed to Jesus saying, "Look, the Lamb of God." "The first thing Andrew did was to find his brother, Simon, and tell him, *'We have found the Messiah' (that is, the Christ). And he brought him to Jesus'*" (Jn 1:41).

After Philip became a disciple of Jesus, he immediately found his friend, Nathaniel, and told him, *"We have found the one Moses wrote about in the Law, and about whom the prophets also wrote – Jesus of Nazareth, the son of Joseph"* When Nathaniel had doubts whether anything good could come from Nazareth, Philip replied, *"Come and see"* (Jn 1:45-46).

Importance of Witnessing: The importance of witnessing is found in Romans 10:9-17 *ESV:*

> *...if you confess with your mouth that Jesus is Lord*
> *and believe in your heart that God raised him from the dead,*
> *you will be saved.*
> *For with the heart one believes and is justified,*
> *and with the mouth one confesses and is saved.*
> *For the Scripture says,*
> *'Everyone who believes in him will not be put to shame'...*
> *For 'everyone who calls on the name of the Lord will be saved.'*
> *How then will they call on him in whom they have not believed?*
> *And how are they to believe in him of whom they have never heard?*
> *And how are they to hear without someone preaching?*
> *And how are they to preach unless they are sent? As it is written,*

'How beautiful are the feet of those who preach the good news!'...
So faith comes from hearing, and hearing through the word of Christ.
Confessing our faith in Jesus naturally follows a heart-felt faith in Christ.
Secret believers are not the norm. Believers share their faith.

Furthermore, those outside of Christ are eternally lost. They have no hope without someone witnessing to them. *"How are they to hear without someone preaching?"*

Do not be confused by the words "preach" and "preaching." You need not think of someone in a clerical garb standing behind a pulpit preaching. The Greek word simply means "to announce, to make known by a herald, to proclaim aloud." You don't need a Bible School education to "preach" nor do you need to stand behind a pulpit.

What every believer can do and should do is to announce and declare in audible words the Good News of Jesus Christ. Tell others what Jesus Christ has done for you. Share the Good News that brought you to faith in Christ. How else will unbelievers know if you don't tell them?

When you tell others what Christ has done for you and share the Good News of Jesus, three things happen: (1) God is pleased and honoured for you have obeyed his call on your life; (2) Others will hear the Good News of the Saviour and by his grace may be saved from their sins as well; (3) And in turn your faith is strengthened. You not only bless others, but you yourself will be blessed. Christians grow stronger in the Lord when they actively share their faith with others.

Exercising by Combating the Evil One

A born again Christian is a child of God, an heir of God and a joint heir with Christ (Ro 8:14-17). Because of this relationship with Christ, believers have every right to live without fear – fear of the unknown, fear of the spirits and fear of death.

But Christians must also face another reality. We live in a world where *"Your enemy the devil prowls around like a roaring lion looking for someone to devour"* (Ja 5:8). We live in a culture that is hostile to God, for the Bible says:

Don't love the world's ways. Don't love the world's goods.
Love of the world squeezes out love for the Father.
Practically everything that goes on in the world –
wanting your own way,
wanting everything for yourself,
wanting to appear important –
has nothing to do with the Father. It just isolates you from him.
The world and all its wanting, wanting, wanting is on the way out –

but whoever does what God wants is set for eternity
(1 Jn 2:15-17 The MESSAGE).

In this mix of a hostile environment (the devil and the world – expressed in human culture) is our own flesh, a fallen sinful nature that is attracted to the sinful elements of our culture. Temptations may come from outside, but sin always is due to inside yielding. Don't blame the devil for your sin; blame yourself, for the Bible says: *"Each one is tempted when, by his own evil desire, he is dragged away and enticed"* (Jas 1:14). For that reason it is important to keep on growing stronger and stronger in faith by the means of grace mentioned above.

In addition, God has provided spiritual weapons to resist the devil and all temptations that come our way.

In conclusion, be strong –
not in yourselves but in the Lord, in the power of his boundless resource.
Put on God's complete armour
so that you can successfully resist all the devil's methods of attack.
For our fight is not against any physical enemy:
It is against organizations and powers that are spiritual.
We are up against the unseen power that controls this dark world,
and spiritual agents from the very headquarters of evil.
Therefore you must wear the whole armour of God
that you may be able to resist evil in its day of power,
and that even when you have fought to a stand-still
you may still stand your ground.
Take your stand then with truth as your belt,
righteousness your breastplate,
the gospel of peace firmly on your feet,
salvation as your helmet
and in your hand the sword of the Spirit, the Word of God.
Above all be sure to take faith as your shield,
for it can quench every burning missile the enemy hurls at you.
Pray at all times with every kind of spiritual prayer,
keeping alert and persistent as you pray for all Christ's men and women
(Eph 6:10-18 Phillips)

Christians are engaged in a fight with evil powers (the world, flesh and the devil). The Greek word for *fight* is a word taken from the root verb, "to throw" or "to swing." It refers to a contest between two persons until one hurls the other down and holds him down. It is a "face to face conflict" to the finish.

However, the Christian need not fear because God has provided the armour needed to win. The Christian's strength is "in the Lord." Notice that each piece of the armour is provided by God. Here the armour is described.

(1) **"The helmet of salvation"** protects the head which is the most vital part of the body. In Christ the believer is saved and sealed by the Holy Spirit. It is vitally important for the believer to know and be assured in his heart that his sins have been forgiven and that he need not fear any future condemnation.

(2) **"The breastplate of righteousness"** protects the second most vital part of the body, the vital organs in the chest. "Righteousness" may be understood both objectively and subjectively. Every person, who has confessed their faith in Christ, has been declared righteous by God – he is justified. God himself has made this pronouncement. This verdict will never be overturned. In God's sight the believer is indwelled by the Holy Spirit who marks and seals the believer as God's very own child. This is based, not on what the person does but on the death of Christ which paid for the sins committed.

Subjectively, however, believers need to live righteous lives, not in order to be saved from damnation, but to be saved from a guilty conscience which will weaken him in the spiritual battle. Sensitivity to sin and confession of sin is important so that the fight can be focused and successful.

(3) **"The belt of truth"** may also be considered both objectively and subjectively. The believer lives with the full confidence in the objective truth of the Good News. God cannot lie. The believer stands tall and strong in the conflict in his confidence in Jesus Christ who is the Truth. But he must also live and tell the truth at all times. Lying and deceiving will only weaken the believer and provide the devil with a weak spot to attack. Always live the truth and tell the truth.

(4) **"The sword of the Spirit"** is the Word of God. The other pieces of the armour are defensive armour to protect the body. But the sword is an offensive weapon. With the sword of the Spirit we defeat the enemy. Each time Satan tempted Jesus, his reply was the quotation of Scripture, *"it is written"* (Mt 4:4,7,10). The believer who dwells in the Scripture is empowered to resist all temptation.

(5) **"The feet fitted with the readiness that comes from the gospel of peace"** is a picture of a soldier of Jesus Christ who uses his feet to take the Good News of Christ to those who need it. The best defense against the devil is a good offense – being prepared to move here

and there with a witness to God's saving grace. A Christian who knows the Scripture and actively witnesses to his faith becomes a strong Christian, able to resist temptation.

(6) **"The shield of faith"** protects from all kinds of "flaming arrows."

Soldiers in ancient times attacked their enemies with arrows tipped with flaming fire. Roman soldiers protected themselves with large leather shields reaching from the feet to the eyes. These shields were soaked in water to quench the fiery arrows. Living faith in God is like a shield able to quench the fiery attacks of the enemy.

One of Satan's clever tactics is to sow seeds of doubt with questions like these: Does God really love me? Is God really able to help me? Why doesn't God answer my prayer? All kinds of questions and doubts may arise which can lead to defeat.

That is how the whole sin problem began in the Garden of Eden. *"Did God really say, 'you must not eat from any tree in the garden'?"* Once doubt in God's trustworthiness was entertained, Eve fell into active disobedience. Strong faith is essential in victory and this faith comes through the Word of God which is the "sword of the Spirit."

(7) **"Pray in the Spirit"** is integral to all victory over temptation. In our anguish we cry out for help, but human words are inadequate, so the Holy Spirit prays for us with groans which words cannot express. We don't even know how we should pray. We read:

The Spirit helps us in our weakness.
We do not know what we ought to pray for,
but the Spirit himself intercedes for us
with groans that words cannot express...
the Spirit intercedes for the saints in accordance with God's will
(Ro 8:26-27).

As we pray in the Spirit, we are assured that the Spirit himself is interceding for us, not with human languages, but with groans that convey meaning beyond human language. So the Spirit assists us by his praying even while we ourselves are praying.

CONCLUSION

If a person neglects healthy food and proper exercise, the body becomes weak and sickly. In like manner, if a Christian neglects to breathe properly by praying and disregards daily feeding on God's Word, that Christian will decline in spiritual vigor. When the leadership of a local congregation or a denomination fails to breathe constantly in prayer and feed faithfully on

God's Word, that church will fall into major problems with the flesh taking over.

Temptations and problems are inevitable. Muscles need to be strengthened in order to resist evil and to persevere in the Christian life. By exercising faith in the spiritual discipline of abiding in Christ, fruit will be borne. By sharing your testimony with others and resisting the devil's temptations with the armour of God, a healthy, vibrant and fruitful Christian will grow into admirable maturity.

God has granted to his children an additional provision to help believers overcome fear of sickness and death – the blessed hope of Christ's return and the resurrection of the body. This is the topic of the last chapter.

7

ANTICIPATING
THE BLESSED HOPE
OF THE BELIEVER

Physical death is inevitable until the Lord returns. Those who have been born again by the Spirit of God have been raised from spiritual death and granted new life in Christ. They will never suffer eternal death, eternal separation from God in hell. But believers do die physically "in Christ" as a consequence of sin.

What is physical death? Traditionally, a person is considered dead if the heart stops beating and breathing ceases. But doctors today cannot agree when death actually occurs because death seems to be in stages and can be reversed. Today death is generally determined when the brain appears dead by the use of an electroencephalogram (EEG).

From the biblical perspective, though the body dies, the person as spirit continues on after death. Death for believers is spoken of as "sleep" in the New Testament. When Lazarus "died," Jesus told his disciples, "Our friend Lazarus has fallen asleep" (Jn 11:11). When Stephen died as a martyr, the Bible says, "he fell asleep" (Ac 7:60). Physical death is not the end of life for believers. It is only a transition to eternal life beyond the grave. The spirit of the person continues to live on. And our hope is in the promises of God.

THE INTERMEDIATE STATE

The Bible says little about the intermediate life, between death and the bodily resurrection. But several verses express the Christian's hope. They indicate that the spirits of all believer in Jesus Christ are immediately transported into the presence of the Lord. They surely do not go to a place called, "purgatory," for the Bible nowhere speaks of such a place. Nor do they lie in the grave unconscious (sleeping) until the resurrection.

Following are the Scriptures filled with hope, teaching Christians what will happen when they "fall asleep."

When Paul was imprisoned in Rome for the first time, he did not know whether he would be released or die at the hands of his captors. But he faced the unknown, the possibility of death, with great joy and hope, saying, *"For to me, to live is Christ and **to die is gain**"* (Php 1:21). For the apostle Paul, his whole life was centred on and motivated by Jesus Christ – to love him, serve him, worship him, trust him and obey him. "Life is Christ" for the apostle. And what of death? It was gain because he would actually be with Christ.

No doubt this faith was based in part on Christ's words on the cross. On both sides of Jesus hung two thieves. When one thief mocked Jesus, the other thief rebuked him and said: *"Jesus, remember me when you come into your kingdom."* Jesus replied, *"I tell you the truth, today you will be with me in paradise"* (Lk 23:42-43). Immediately, upon the death of this thief, he was in the presence of Jesus in paradise on the basis of his faith in Christ. That was Paul's hope and ours today.

The future of believers after death is blessed. Listen to the apostle John who spoke of the blessing of the "dead who die in the Lord." *"'Yes,' says the Spirit, 'they will rest from their labor, for their deeds will follow them'"* (Rev 14:14). Rest awaits God's people after death and their good works will follow them with the attending reward from God.

One of the most extensive passages in Scripture that deals with death and life after death was written to the Corinthians. What a wonderful blessing it would be if every believer would share in this faith and hope expressed by the apostle. He concludes by saying:

"We know that while we are at home in the body
we are away from the Lord, for we walk by faith, not by sight.
Yes, we are of good courage
and we would rather be away from the body and at home with the Lord.
So whether we are at home or away, we make it our aim to please him
(2 Co 4:16-5:10 ESV).

Instead of being discouraged with his aging, dying body, by faith Paul sees the bright side. The trials and tests in life are God's means of refining, purifying and growing the Christian. What Paul focuses on is not what is seen, but what cannot be seen, the eternal, unseen realities promised by God and purchased for us by Christ on the cross.

This world, filled with suffering, pain and tears, is not the final destination of believers. God is actually preparing us for our bright future and has given us his Spirit who guarantees what God has promised. Have you trusted in Christ to save you from your sins? If so, the Spirit of God lives in you, and he guarantees every believer that what is mortal (our tents – physical bodies – filled with all kinds of sickness and eventual death) will be swallowed up with life.

Whether Paul lives in this world or is away from his earthly body, he says, *"We make it our aim to please him."* He says this in part because of the certainty that after death we shall all appear before "the judgement seat of Christ" to receive the rewards awaiting the believer who served God faithfully on this earth. No one who has been justified by faith should fear condemnation (Ro 8:1). Jesus paid that debt on Calvary. But Christians are called to be faithful in living for Christ, using their spiritual gifts for the glory of God who will reward his faithful servants.

The Christian life is comparable to a person running a marathon – a life long race. Africans, especially Kenyans and Ethiopians, are world famous for their marathon champions. The Greek young men trained diligently and ran energetically in order to win a crown of laurel leaves that soon wilted, dried up and disintegrated. But a Christian should run the marathon race of life with the same diligence in order to receive "*a crown that will last forever*" (1 Co 9:24-27).

The pastors and elders of the church were challenged by Peter to be faithful "shepherds of God's flock" so that when the Chief Shepherd appears they would receive "*the crown of glory that will never fade away*" (1 Pe 5:1-4).

A self-centred Christian who does not seek to be faithful to God will lose the blessings awaiting the faithful.

Do you truly want deliverance from the fear of sickness and death? The Psalmist wrote, "*I have hidden your word in my heart that I might not sin against you*" (Ps 119:11). To fear sickness and death is unbelief, doubting the promises of God, for the Bible says: "*And everything that does not come from faith is sin*" (Ro 14:23). The best way to deal with fears and doubts is to memorize the Word of God. Memorizing 2 Corinthians 4:16-5:10 will surely generate faith and hope for the future.

THE BLESSED HOPE

Most people have hope for one thing or another, but their hope is like a kite that flies upward and then hurtles toward the earth, ever buffeted with the winds. When circumstances are encouraging, hope is strong. But when discouragements sweep over the soul, hope wanes and fades.

Certainty of our Hope

Hope is important in this world. If hope is the feeling that events will turn out for the best, then hope is necessary for anyone to live. Given all the pain and suffering of this world, why continue to live if all hope is lost? Because the world is without any sure hope of life after death, their philosophy is natural: "*Let us eat and drink, for tomorrow we die*" (1 Co 15:32).

When unbelievers die, many wail and cry with shrieks of hopelessness, others grieve quietly and a few remain stoic in denial. As the Bible teaches, they are a people *"without hope"* (Eph 2:12).

In a sense traditional Africans had hope. They hoped for prosperity in this world through the mystical powers of magic and witchcraft. They even had hope of continued life after death for four or five generations when they would be remembered by name. But what a hope was this! Women, children and unmarried Africans had no hope for they lacked any status in society. Those who were influential and powerful in this life expected to have the same status in the next life, a life similar to the present life with jealousies and power struggles. Eventually, everyone would fade from the memories of the living and become mere "its," nameless spirits who would be feared by the living.

If all others lack a sure hope, what of Christians? Of all people, Christians have a certain hope. If Christians have no hope of a future resurrection, they are worse off than unbelievers. Non-Christians indulge in the pleasures of sin for a season, but the believer denies himself and takes up his cross and follows Jesus. As the Bible says, *"If only for this life we have hope in Christ, we are to be pitied more than all men"* (1 Co 15:19).

But the Bible teaches that Christians do have a sure hope. Their hope is grounded in the Lord Jesus Christ. The Bible teaches, *"Christ Jesus [is] our hope"* (1 Ti 1:1). *"Christ in you, the hope of glory"* (Col 1:27).

Our hope is based on the certainty of Jesus' resurrection. Because Jesus lives, all fear is gone – or, it should be gone. Think of the evidence for Jesus' resurrection!

(1) We have multiple eye witnesses who saw Jesus after his resurrection. Many doubted at first until they met with him personally. They touched him, saw him eat and heard him speak.

(2) We have five written eye-witness accounts of his resurrection, four written 30 years after the resurrection and John written after 40-50 years.

(3) We know these resurrection accounts are accurate for many reasons. The first witnesses to the resurrected Jesus, according to all accounts in the Bible, were women. But the male dominated society in Jesus' day did not accept the creditability of a woman's testimony. Since the testimony of women was not believed in their culture, no one, who would want to fabricate the resurrection of Jesus, would have given credit to the women who first testified of his resurrection.

(4) These eye witnesses testified to Jesus' resurrection in Jerusalem immediately after the resurrection and were never refuted by anyone.

(5) Most of his apostles, separately and on different occasions, died for their testimony of Jesus. Who would be willing to die for a lie that they had concocted? "Doubting Thomas," who refused to believe that Jesus arose from the dead until he met him and put his fingers into the nail prints in his hands, traveled to India as a missionary and was martyred for his testimony.

(6) The miraculous spread of the Christian Church in the face of extreme persecution during the first 200 years verifies the supernatural truths of the Christian Gospel that Jesus died, rose again from the dead and ascended into heaven from where he poured out the Holy Spirit to grow the Church.

For Christians our blessed hope is certain for the Bible teaches: "_We have this hope as an anchor for the soul, **firm and secure**. It enters the inner sanctuary behind the curtain, where Jesus, who went before us, has entered on our behalf. He has become a high priest forever, in the order of Melchizedek_" (Heb 6:19f).

Anchors of a ship drop down to the ocean bed, holding fast the ship from the surging sea. The believer's anchor reaches into "the inner sanctuary behind the curtain" where Jesus dwells and intercedes for us. Jesus Christ saved us by his death 2,000 years ago, but today he continues his work of salvation through his intercession on our behalf. By faith our anchor is secured to God himself, the faithful God who always keeps his promises.

The Christian life is one of a personal relationship with the Triune God. Only as we develop this relationship through a life of prayer and meditation on God's Word, can our faith be strengthened. Because of our relationship with Jesus Christ, we can be assured of our future hope.

The Second Advent

The hope we have of being with Christ immediately upon death is not our ultimate hope. After death we will be alive with Christ, but without our resurrected bodies. The intermediate state between death and the resurrection is not our ultimate destiny.

At the First Advent Christ came as a tiny infant child, laid in a manger, and unrecognized by most as the Son of God. When Christ returns again he will come in his majestic splendour as the reigning Monarch, the Messiah – the Greater Son of David, the sovereign King of kings and Lord of lords. This coming is our "blessed hope" (Tit 2:13) because we will at that time be raised from the dead with resurrected bodies and everything will change.

The time of the Second Advent is not known, although the signs preceding his coming indicate that Jesus is returning soon (Mt 24:3-14, 36).

Christ will return personally, bodily and visibly just as Christ ascended to heaven bodily and visibly (Ac 1:9ff).

His coming will be noisy "with a loud command, with the voice of the archangel and with the trumpet call of God" (1 Th 4:16).

To encourage each person with the Blessed Hope and the resurrection of the dead, we shall consider two passages of Scripture.

I tell you this, brothers:
flesh and blood cannot inherit the kingdom of God,
nor does the perishable inherit the imperishable.
Behold! I tell you a mystery.
We shall not all sleep, but we shall all be changed,
in a moment, in the twinkling of an eye, at the last trumpet.
For the trumpet will sound,
and the dead will be raised imperishable, and we shall be changed.
For this perishable body must put on the imperishable,
and this mortal body must put on immortality.
When the perishable puts on the imperishable
and the mortal puts on immortality,
then shall come to pass the saying that is written:
"Death is swallowed up in victory."
"O Death, where is your victory?"
"O death, where is your sting?"
The sting of death is sin, and the power of sin is the law.
But thanks be to God,
who gives us the victory through our Lord Jesus Christ.
Therefore, my beloved brothers, be steadfast, immovable,
always abounding in the work of the Lord,
knowing that in the Lord your labor is not in vain
(1 Co 15:50-58 *ESV*).

We have seen that when the believer dies, the real person, his spirit, ascends immediately into the presence of the Lord while his body gives way to corruption and decay in the earth. At the moment of death and in the presence of the Lord the believer's old sinful nature is cast off and he is restored to being a perfectly sinless, holy person, for the Bible teaches, "...*we shall be like him, for we shall see him as he is*" (1 Jn 3:2).

But our redemption is not yet complete because we have not yet received our resurrected bodies. God created Adam and Eve and all their posterity to be body, soul and spirit. Without a body, a human being is not complete.

Paul wrote, "...*we ourselves, who have the firstfruits of the Spirit, groan inwardly as we wait eagerly for our adoption as sons, the redemption of our bodies*" (Ro 8:23). Our salvation is in several stages. The last stage is the "redemption of our bodies." Christians are already adopted as children of God, but our inheritance is not complete until we receive our resurrected bodies.

In the passage quoted above (1 Co 15:50-58), Scripture declares that our present perishable bodies of flesh and blood cannot inherit the kingdom of God. This will all change when Christ returns for the Bible says: *"We shall all be changed, in a moment, in the twinkling of an eye, at the last trumpet. For the trumpet will sound, and the dead will be raised imperishable, and we shall be changed"* (1 Co 15:51b-52).

What kind of body will it be? Paul explains that it will be a different kind of a body; it will be a body like Christ has, for *"we shall be like him."* Jesus could be recognized. The nail prints in his hands and the gash in his side remained. He could eat like he did in the past, but he could also pass through walls.

The resurrected bodies of believers are called "spiritual" bodies (1 Co 15:42-44). They will be imperishable, glorious and powerful. *"Just as we have borne the image of the man of dust, we shall also bear the image of the man of heaven* (1 Co 15:49). Our bodies will be like the body of Jesus.

The Second Coming of Christ is "blessed" because at that moment, *"death is swallowed up in victory."* Death has reigned since the Fall of Adam and Eve. With the first coming of the Second Adam (Jesus), the doom of all evil creatures was sealed on the cross, ensuring that death together with all evil creatures will be finally judged at the second coming. By faith we believers can shout with joy to the Lord:

"Death is swallowed up in victory."
"O Death, where is your victory?"
"O death, where is your sting?"
The sting of death is sin, and the power of sin is the law.
But thanks be to God,
who gives us the victory through our Lord Jesus Christ.

With this blessed hope, believers ought to shout with victory when faced with sickness and death. By faith we have seen what Christ did at his first coming, and by faith we trust him to bring final victory at his second coming.

Therefore, during the remaining days and years of our lives, we need to be *"steadfast, immovable, always abounding in the work of the Lord, knowing that in the Lord [our] labor is not in vain"* (1 Co 15:50). We walk by faith and not by sight.

The Christians in Thessalonica were concerned about their loved ones who had fallen asleep in the Lord. What would happen to them? In the above quoted passage Paul explains the initial events that will occur at the Second Advent.

> *But we do not want you to be uninformed, brothers,*
> *about those who are asleep,*
> *that you may not grieve as others do who have no hope.*
> *For since we believe that Jesus died and rose again, even so,*
> *through Jesus, God will bring with him those who have fallen asleep.*
> *For this we declare to you by a word from the Lord,*
> *that we who are alive, who are left until the coming of the Lord,*
> *will not precede those who have fallen asleep.*
> *For the Lord himself will descend from heaven with a cry of command,*
> *with the voice of an archangel, and with the sound of the trumpet of God.*
> *And the dead in Christ will rise first.*
> *Then we who are alive, who are left, will be*
> *caught up together with them in the clouds to meet the Lord in the air,*
> *and so we will always be with the Lord.*
> *Therefore, encourage on another with these words*
> (1 Th 4:13-18 ESV).

The departed believers will not be left behind. In fact, the dead in Christ will rise first with their resurrected bodies. Then Christians who are alive at Christ's coming will also be transformed and ascend together with the departed saints and they will be raptured (caught up) together to meet the Lord in the air.

This Good News should remove all fear and doubts. We need to encourage ourselves with these words. Christians are saved by faith and they continue to grow in the Lord by faith. As their faith is strengthened by the Word of God, they find that God removes all fear from their hearts.

CONCLUSION

Fear, the kind of fear described as terror, dread, worry, anxiety, horror, fright, alarm, and apprehension, is a consequence of sin. In heaven reverential fear of God prevails but bathed in loving adoration, joy and peace. In the Garden of Eden, fashioned by God on earth, everything was good. Anxiety did not exist.

But when Adam and Eve sinned, anxiety entered the human race. Adam and Eve were afraid and hid from God (Ge 3:10). God's punishment was death, just as God had warned. *"By the sweat of your brow you will eat your food until you return to the ground, since from it you were taken; for dust you are and to dust you will return"* (Ge 3:19).

Ever since that first sin, the human race has been *"through fear of death were subject to slavery all their lives"* (Heb 2:15). Fear of death is universally experienced. Africans are no exceptions.

The resolution of this problem is a restored relationship with God. Men and women seek to please God and qualm their conscience by trying to live a good life. The problem is that our sinful human nature is unable to live a perfect life and our conscience convicts us of falling short.

Martin Luther, a devout Catholic Christian, was terrified during a thunder storm and feared death. Crying out to God for help, he promised God that he would enter a monastery if he were spared death. During his years as an Augustinian monk, he tried desperately hard to do what was right, following all the monastic regulations, observing all the pious duties of prayer and confession of his sins to his superior. But his conscience gave him no peace. He began to hate God for his righteous demands which he could not fulfill. His heart was filled with guilt and fear.

All this changed when Martin Luther discovered from Scripture that *"the just shall live by faith."* Forgiveness of sins is offered, not by keeping the law, but by God's gracious gift to all who believe in Jesus. Forgiveness of sins cannot be earned or merited by human effort. Forgiveness and being made right with God was a gift of grace. God's righteousness is imputed (credited or assigned) to everyone who *believes* in Jesus who paid the penalty for our sin on the cross.

When anyone receives this gracious gift by faith, he or she is justified, declared righteous and clothed in righteousness. The cause of fear has been removed for the believer has been made right with God. Sickness and death are no more enemies to be feared. Growing into mature Christians strengthens faith and replaces fear with joyful hope and calm assurance.

The capstone which secures our hope is the resurrection of Christ from the dead. Not only did Christ die in our place to secure our redemption, he arose from the dead and ascended to heaven where he intercedes for us before the Father (Ro 8:27, 34).

The great victory of Christ over sin, death and all evil was made possible by the crucifixion **and** resurrection of Christ. Because Christ died **and** rose again, we can face tomorrow with joy and confidence.

In the words of a hymn composed by Gloria and William Gaither, we close this book.

"God sent His Son, they called Him Jesus,
"He came to love, heal and forgive;
"He lived and died to buy my pardon,
"An empty grave is there to prove my Saviour lives.

"Because He lives I can face tomorrow,
"**Because He lives all fear is gone**;
"Because I know He holds the future.
"And life is worth the living just because He lives

"And then one day I'll cross the river,
"I'll fight life's final war with pain;
"And then as death gives way to victory,
"I'll see the lights of glory and I'll know He lives.

"Because He lives I can face tomorrow,
"**Because He lives, all fear is gone**;
"Because I know He holds the future.
"And life is worth the living just because He lives."

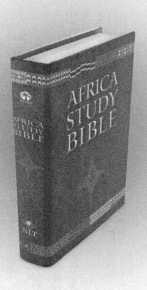

Experience the truth and beauty
of *God's Word Through African Eyes.*

With notes written by over **350 contributors** from **50 countries** in **five major languages**, the *Africa Study Bible*™ is a collaboration of scholars, leaders, pastors, and teachers from across the continent, who together created **the most ethnically diverse, one-volume, biblical resource to date.**

Discover more at **africastudybible.com**.

OASIS INTERNATIONAL LIMITED
Satisfying Africa's Thirst for God's Word

africastudybible.com
facebook.com/africastudybible
info@oasisint.net

NLT.
The Truth Made
CLEAR

OASIS INTERNATIONAL LTD
is the proud publisher
of many great titles to help inform your Christian life!
Check these out!

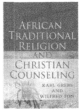

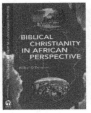

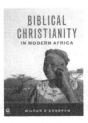
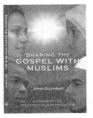

Made in the USA
Monee, IL
07 October 2021

79570247R00066